Al

94 Morris St

West HAVEN CT

06516

Boathouse Days

-ROBE

Boathouse Days

Inwood-on-Hudson
in the 1930s

R E Roberts

Copyright © 2001 by R E Roberts.

Library of Congress Number: 2001116082
ISBN #:   Hardcover   0-7388-6138-3
               Softcover   0-7388-6137-5

This book was printed in the United States of America.

To order additional copies of this book, contact:
Xlibris Corporation
1-888-7-XLIBRIS
www.Xlibris.com
Orders@Xlibris.com

Contents

1| Preface

THIS IS THE story of a place and a time—and of a family who lived in that place at that time.

To begin with I had to shine a searchlight into the past to find out where I lived and what my life was like there. From where I stood, all I could see was a neighborhood in decay: blocks of dirty streets with vacant lots and aging apartment buildings; double-parked cars; an unkempt park with fallen trees blocking disintegrating paths and, below it, a deserted river front.

Then I detected a glint from the jewels of the past when I thought about the circumstances of my own time. At that point I asked myself what made this time and place so special to me. And that's when the magic and the mystery began to unfold. Surely, this place where I lived out those first seventeen years of my life holds not only the traces of my own time, but yet another, and another before that.

Eventually it became clear why this singular setting suddenly took on such importance. This wasn't just my first home—a place of first impressions, the place where I spent the growing-up years of my life. With the perspective of advanced years, I understood now my brief tenancy in Inwood in an entirely new context. I suddenly realized that I carried deep inside me the matrix of eons of habitation. I began to gather in the message of my folk genes. The sensation intrigued me.

To anyone who stops to think about it, there is something haunting, maybe even sacred, about a place where untold numbers of people have lived before. Popularly, this is most often associated with a house. But it could just as well be a town or a city, or a section of a large city—like Inwood.

Maybe it all begins with the geography of the place. Suggested by the face of the land, someone has given the place a name: Shor-a-kap-kok, T'Ubrecht's Hoek, Mt. Washington, Cold Spring, or Inwood-on-Hudson. But the name is really only a part of a phenomenon I'll call for now, Propriety Succession.

By common acceptance, the place I speak of will by name, use, and reputation come to have an identity and character all its own. This uniqueness is created by something more than the shape of the land, a name, or the people who live there. It comes not only from the place as it is now, but as surely from what it was then. Most of the present inhabitants will be only dimly aware of this cultural residue (as I once was) although it is their inheritance.

In this context it's not hard to imagine that my particular place would have a collective soul—if one considers that a succession of living beings occupied this same plot of land at some earlier time, and that all of them left something of themselves behind. The succession, as you would expect, is ongoing. New people come along and take up residence in the hills and valleys and shorelines I once roamed. They take what was passed along to them, use it as they see fit and make their own contributions to it.

I accepted without quarrel the place that was assigned to me for the term of my occupancy. I adopted the institutions of that time and place and would be shaped by them. When I left, I went forward with the stamp of these things on me. And when I left, I would leave behind the remnants of them and of me for my successors to discover.

2| Awakening

"BUY . . . CASH . . . CLOTHES!" Only the strong consonants and stylized vowels floated up to the apartment windows: "Baa . . . Kah . . . Klo!" I was drawn to the street cry of the pushcart peddler. The hoarse call echoed in the canyon between the sets of five and six-story apartment buildings that lined each side of the hill up Seaman Avenue from Dyckman Street and found their way up to our new third floor apartment.

It was 1928 and I was three years old. My mind was fresh and alert, but the new sounds didn't connect somehow. I sensed that there must be a different world down there in the streets, a world full of wonderment and excitement. These were sounds that went beyond my experience and even my mother's blunt explanation: "Oh, it's just the old Jew rag picker." They preached the message of a coarser fabric of life. Here was energy encoded into some special new language. It was designed to command attention, and it spoke directly for itself and for a way of life I knew nothing about.

The apartment house we had just moved into, 2 Seaman Avenue, began the Block. Seaman Avenue rose up from the canyon of Dyckman Street and leveled off momentarily for Cumming Street on the right which ran back down to Broadway. Then Seaman climbed to another stage to Beak Street on the left. This was little more than the suggestion of a street that was finally paved over and given its name when the newer apartments facing the park were built in the late thirties. The sixty or so yards of Beak

Street ended at Payson Avenue, and at this juncture rose the undisturbed, almost secret wooded heights of Inwood Hill Park.

There was an entrance to the Park here. It was an old Indian trail that led to the summit of what was known of old as the Green Hill. Then it went back down to the site of the Great Tulip Tree. Stretching out from the ancient tulip tree was the Spouting Meadow for which Spuyten Duyvil was really named. (The usual mistranslation of the Old Dutch name was In Spite of the Devil, solidified by Washington Irving's fanciful Knickerbocker legend written of the region.) Here, where Spuyten Duyvil Creek flowed, where Henry Hudson was believed to have dropped the Half Moon's anchor, on the Manhattan side there once was an Indian village called Shora-kap-kok. It spread out along the flats and under the hills, just below the present site of the Henry Hudson Bridge. Some idea of what the village must have looked like is revealed by the model constructed by the Museum of the American Indian based on excavations made in the 1920s.

Payson Avenue bordered Inwood Hill Park along its entire length. Where Beak Street ended, it began its descent to Dyckman Street by a series of two-story, red-brick homes. One of these had been occupied by the Weiss family whose illustrious relation was better known by the name of Houdini, escape artist and illusionist.

But before Payson Avenue reached the Dyckman valley, there was a wider entrance to the Park. It was a road, not signposted, but commonly known to residents as Bolton Road. It got its name from two wealthy brothers, owners of a fleet of clipper ships, who bought Inwood Hill a century before for a wood lot. The brothers also built a limestone quarry by the shores of the original Spuyten Duyvil Creek, which eventually came to be known as Marble Hill. Bolton Road wound up to the summit of the Park, and until the mid nineteen-thirties, offered access to the old Dyckman Library and the original Jewish Memorial Hospital. Farther up Bolton Road was the House of Mercy, a home for "wayward girls" and homeless children. Then came the House of Rest, twin houses which offered shelter for "helpless sufferers" Further yet, overlooking the Hudson River Railway tracks was the home of James McCreery, a department store magnate. And at the very top of the park was the site of the old Revolutionary War Cock Hill Fort.

Two more six-story apartment buildings completed the Payson Avenue run downhill to Dyckman Street. The upper one was elegantly titled "The Charles;" the next, just plain 1-49 Payson Avenue.

A broad apron of sidewalk along Dyckman Street between Payson Avenue and Seaman Avenue closed the long and hilly rectangle of the Block. Under the apartment buildings there was a line of storefronts: Lippman's pharmacy, Katzenberg's tailor shop, a speakeasy, the Profetta Brothers' barbershop, Moe's (later Irv's) newsstand and candy store, and the Lorraine Pharmacy and luncheonette.

These storefront proprietors, buyers and sellers of goods and services, inevitably were home to the kind of turmoil and confusion that breathe life into a community: "Boy-us, boy-us! Dun't play by deh sto' vindeh!" shouted Lippman, flapping his white-coated arms at us. It was the cry of the street peddler all over again. It wouldn't be long before I'd come to understand the rhythms and the nuances.

Dyckman Street and the Block with its shadowy hill-park was the first territory deeded to me. It was the place where I began the early lessons of life. I took it in without question. I used it and enjoyed it and, as is most often the case, outgrew it and moved on.

3| BOATHOUSE 1

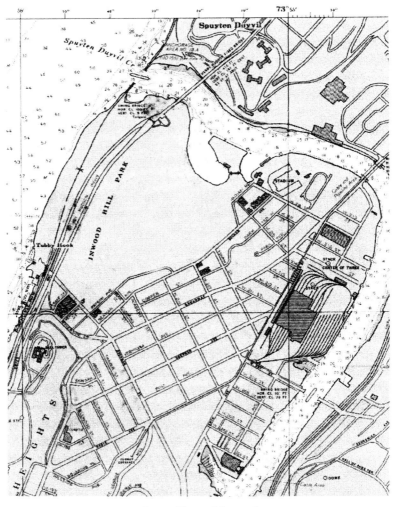

River Chart of Inwood

THE BOATHOUSE THAT was about to become my home was built along Hudson's river in the northern Manhattans around the turn of the 20th century by a man named George Smith. The original structure was a two-story, wood-frame house that projected out over the river just south of Dyckman Street, or Inwood Street as it was called then. Smith's boathouse sometime later became the home of the Spuyten Duyvil Boat and Canoe Club. Soon after, the name, "West's Boathouse" was appended reflecting the name of its new owner.

The house was supported above the water by rock-filled, railroad-tie cribs. Canoes lined the open floor passageway from the shoreline entrance to the outer decking over the river where a gangway was pinned. The gangway led down to a float moored at its corners by four tall shorn tree stakes. The gangway rolled on wide iron wheels as the float rose and fell from the normal three foot tidal range every six hours or so. Or, as it was heaved about by the waves from the day liners, the *Peter Stuyvesant*, the *DeWitt Clinton*, or the newer *Alexander Hamilton*.

The upper story of the house contained rudimentary living quarters: a bedroom, a kitchen, a small living room and a front room that looked out over the river. Some fifty feet back from the land filled shoreline ran the old Hudson River Railway, later a division of the New York Central Railroad. From the kitchen window one could watch the hundred-car freight trains rumble noisily by.

Before it was filled in for the railroad, the cove where the Boathouse now stood had been known as the Little Sand Bay. It had long been a favorite fishing ground for the Indians and later, for the white settlers of New Harlem. Some two-hundred yards to the north along the river's edge once nestled the tiny village of Tubby Hook. Though the name was lost, even to the residents of my day, it is still preserved on river charts.

4| Penadnic/Tubby Hook/

Mt. Washington/Inwood

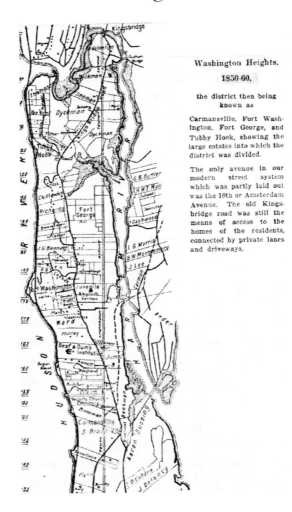

Washington Heights,
1850-60,

the district then being
known as

Carmansville, Fort Washington, Fort George, and Tubby Hook, showing the large estates into which the district was divided.

The only avenue in our modern street system which was partly laid out was the 10th or Amsterdam Avenue. The old Kingsbridge road was still the means of access to the homes of the residents, connected by private lanes and driveways.

DURING THE FIRST to middle years of the 19th century the tiny village of Tubby Hook was localized at a prominent point of land jutting out into the Hudson River. The small community soon ranged inland along what eventually became Inwood Street and later, Dyckman Street over its entire length. The road, to begin with, was no more than a rudimentary thoroughfare between the ridge of hills overlooking the Hudson. It crossed the King's Bridge Road (today's Broadway) at the same time as it joined another road leading up to the Riverside Drive. At this axial location, in 1846, the Mount Washington Church opened its doors for the first time to serve the Tubby Hook and the Mount Washington communities.

Church and Revolutionary War records help to explain the diversity of names for the area. Writes the Rev. Walter D. Knight in 1932 in a booklet called "The Story of Mount Washington—1844-1932":

> This latter name (Tubby Hook), it appears, was originally given to the point of land which juts out into the Hudson just below Spuyten Duyvil Creek. This curious name, was given to that point because, before the railroad bridge obstructed the view, to one passing on the Hudson River the little bay in the creek resembled a tub, the high hills forming its sides and the water in the bay its bottom.
>
> Mount Washington, in the Church records, applies only to the territory now known as Inwood Hill Park in which Mr. Thomson's (founder and Church Elder) residence formerly stood. As late as 1854 this name is recorded in connection with members coming from that hill; but about that time it began to give way to the more general name Tubby Hook, which, in turn, yielded to Inwood. In the records of the Revolution appears a letter from General Washington to General Greene dated White Plains, Nov. 8, 1776, in which, referring to the evacuation of Fort Washington, the Commander-in-Chief says: "I am inclined to think it will not be prudent to hazard the men and stores at Mount Washington, but, as you are on the spot, leave it to you to give such orders as to evacuation."

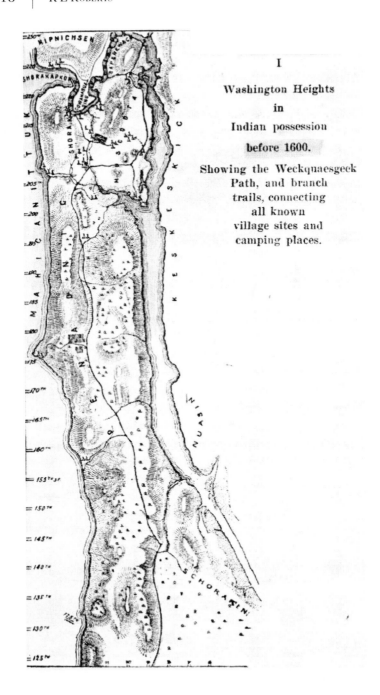

I

Washington Heights

in

Indian possession

before 1600.

Showing the Weckquaesgeck
Path, and branch
trails, connecting
all known
village sites and
camping places.

It is plain, then, that in 1800 the term Mount Washington was the popular name for the whole range of hills extending from Manhattanville to Spuyten Duyvil Creek; for the out-works of Fort Washington covered that entire range, one being Fort Tryon, just south of the old Church, and another, Cock Hill Fort, near the former residence of Mr. James McCreery, above the Jewish Hospital, overlooking Spuyten Duyvil Creek.

Until 1854-56 the name lingered on our records in connection with the hill north of Dyckman Street, as well as the range south of it. The Church being in the depression between these two was for a time known as the Mount Washington Valley Church; but the name by which, in 1851, it was legally incorporated was the Mount Washington; a good, old, historic name, worthy of preservation.

Two footnotes add further dimension and some clarification to Dr. Knight's discussion. Penadnic was the name the Indians had given to the "whole range of hills" he refers to. Secondly, Tubby Hook (the inspiration and title of a Knickerbocker poem about the region by Arthur Guiterman that supports the tub-like bay idea) was almost certainly named for an early settler from the lowlands of Brabant who lived there. His name was Ubrecht. He was called Te Ubrecht or T'Ubrecht. The name was some time later clipped and corrupted to Tubby and tied to the little cape of land on which he once lived—so, Tubby Hook.

Church records further define Inwood's rural aspect, its insularity and its slow growth from 1850 to 1900. In 1914, speaking to a Church assembly on the fortieth anniversary of Dr. George Shipman Payson's pastorate, prominent Church Member and later Elder, Charles E. Flitner offers a provocative picture of the Inwood of the mid-1800s:

In my boyhood on the East side of Kingsbridge Road (Broadway) from the line of 187th Street to the Canal

(Ship Canal at Spuyten Duyvil Creek joining the Hudson and Harlem Rivers), there were but seven buildings. Of these the school house (Ward School, later P.S. 52), the gas house, and the Sowerby house are still standing, and even these will soon be only a memory. One road led east from Kingsbridge Road, going to the Century House on the line of 212th Street, and to a private cemetery situated near it. On the west the only road led to the railway station of the Hudson River Railway and a dock at which coal barges landed and schooners from Maine loaded with cord wood and lumber. The name of the railway station had recently been changed from Tubby Hook to Inwood. From this road, almost at its junction with Kingsbridge Road and directly opposite the Church, a shady lane wound up the hill past the quarry of Mr. Geo. Gantz with its cold spring. From the railway station another road led north along the river—'the river road,' and a short distance east of the station a road turned south to Mr. Wm. H. Hays' place following the line of Riverside Drive.

As this community was isolated from the great city, so its social life was unique. From my earliest recollections the social event of the whole year was the winter skating. A brook ran north of Inwood St. (now Dyckman St.), went under Kingsbridge Road and eastward to the Harlem River. About three hundred feet east of Kingsbridge Road it ran between two small hills. Here early in December we built a dam, and by Christmas we generally had an acre or two of good ice. During the rest of the winter nearly the whole community including old men and children gathered on the pond in the evening about the only social life of the community. We assiduously gathered firewood and bought barrels of tar, and on Saturday nights had special illuminations, outrivaling as some of us would maintain, the brilliance of electricity.

In the summer the river was a constant delight and attraction. Our favorite swimming ground was in Spuyten Duyvil Creek beyond Mr. Mc Creery's. Here the boys would gather at high tide for all kinds of swimming 'stunts.' Many of us had boats, and on moonlight nights we would go up or down the river or into Spuyten Duyvil Creek. By day we would take longer excursions, and many delightful all-day trips were made.

In a tribute to Dr. Payson at his retirement delivered before the Presbytery of New York in 1920, Robert R. Perkins, a Member of the Congregation for the full forty-six years of Dr. Payson's pastorate, describes the Inwood of 1874 and the changes that befell the small community over the last quarter of the 19th century:

Old Church

The little Mount Washington Church, located in the Inwood Valley, was the center of a little rural population. On the west was the beautiful Hudson, on the east the less pretentious Harlem, on the north and south were high hills, and scattered here and there upon those hills were the beautiful residences of those who made up his (Dr. Payson's) congregation. Homes of refinement and affluence they were, and among his flock were some of the most prominent and influential people of our city. During those years and under his pastorate, the Mount Washington Church was the banner Church of the Presbytery of New York, giving more per capita to charities and benevolences than any other Church within its bounds. Then, suddenly, a marvelous thing happened. These beautiful homes one by one were deserted, and one of the fairest regions in this state became in a few years a veritable wilderness. The splendid residences were occupied solely, if at all, by caretakers. Instead of a natural increase of the population such as one would expect here on Manhattan Island in the City of New York, there was an actual decrease, so that, for a quarter of a century following, there were only about fifty Protestant families living within two miles of the Church, and these very poor. The place became, as I say, a veritable wilderness, isolated from the rest of our city. There were no means of communication with the exception of a dilapidated branch of the New York Central, which ran an occasional train between Spuyten Duyvil and West 30th Street, provided the fireman or conductor were not otherwise engaged. There was no post office, no telegraph station, no telephone, no electric light—absolutely none of the modern conveniences enjoyed by a rural town. The nearest drug store, the nearest market and the nearest doctor was two or three miles away.

Payson himself records in "Forty Years in the Wilderness," a booklet he published in 1914, the changes that took place in Inwood as the 1800s drew to a close and the new century began:

Recent years have wrought great changes at Inwood. The last decade especially covers its transformations from village simplicity to metropolitan complexity and confusion.

Cable-cars reached Fort George in 1892, but Fort George was a mile and a half away. The Broadway trolley line was laid through Inwood to Kings Bridge in 1900, and then, for the first time, the moribund real estate of Inwood began to show signs of life and slowly to bestir itself. In 1905 subway trains reached Dyckman Street, and subsequently ran to Van Cortlandt Park. Inwood then began to grow; and since then...it has grown rapidly. After 1905 the population increased so much that...there are now living in apartment houses east of Broadway, and between Arden Street and 213th Street, 1,421 families.

In a note of distress Dr. Payson adds: "Commercialism has poisoned the neighborhood already. The city is upon us with its sharp demand for virtuous strife and struggle with multiplied forms of vice." But he goes on to accept this as an added opportunity, indeed responsibility, to provide spiritual sustenance to the community.

The coming of the first subway at the point where Sherman's Creek widened into a bay out to the Harlem River established Dyckman Street as a major thoroughfare. By the 1920s, at its opposite end, the original Inwood Street, now an extension, came to an end at an automobile carrying ferry that crossed the Hudson to Englewood Cliffs, New Jersey. In the 20s and 30s, three to six story apartment houses continued to go up along paved streets all through the vale to the end of the Island where the Harlem River Ship Canal cut short the original meandering Spuyten Duyvil Creek.

In spite of its rapid growth in the early 1900s, Inwood, once seen as a "rus in urbe" by virtue of its protective hills and fertile valley, still retained some of its geographical insularity from the City of New York. City park planner Olmstead, who was responsible for Central Park, with an eye on majestic Inwood Hill Park envisioned the community as "a neighborhood for fairly comfortable people."

5| Missy 1

TO SET THE record straight, Missy's real name was not Melissa or any similar voguish name. It was plain Caroline (Carrie, or "Caa" to her family). It got to be Missy by a fairly common route. The tenants at West's Boathouse, being younger people and taught to be respectful, always addressed her as Mrs. West. This was at the time when I was beginning to talk, and I parroted the name the best way I could. It came out "Missy West," and as so often happens in such cases, the name stuck—at least, the

Missy at Left

front part of it did. Missy didn't like it very much, but she preferred it to any of the other babytalk versions of grandmother including *gammy* or *nana*. Such titles signaled advancing years to her, and Missy never liked to be reminded of how old she was.

Missy was born Caroline Witten in 1878, in the town of Elizabeth, New Jersey. She was of German ancestry, a twin and one of four sisters and a brother. She had a sixth grade education and could read and write about as well as anyone of her sex and humble estate was expected to at that time. She also absorbed a smattering of house-German over her childhood years, and while she couldn't really speak it well, she could understand it. In fact, she never lost an opportunity to try a word or two with a Boathouse tenant who had a German-sounding name.

In 1898, when she was twenty, she gave birth to a son out of wedlock. She named him Theodore after the Rough Rider Roosevelt of San Juan Hill, we supposed. With a little pressure from both families, Theodore's father, Billy Roberts was soon made to put things right. He married Caroline, giving the boy his family name.

It didn't seem to matter that no one had ever thought to register baby Theodore's birth. Years later that little omission caused my father a good deal of anguish when he tried to apply for his Old Age and Survivor's Insurance benefits under the Social Security Act of the second Roosevelt. It appeared that Missy, who was still very much alive at the time, couldn't bring herself to admit the circumstances of her son's birth either to him or to anyone else—any more than she could admit that she secretly smoked cigarettes. When pressed, she insisted she couldn't remember where the non-existent birth certificate was.

This awkward situation left my father with no choice but to flounder around in halls of records, hospitals and churches filling out endless applications and forms. He finally wrung enough information out of Missy to locate the church where he was baptized, and so was able finally to verify his existence, at least insofar as the record was concerned.

Missy and Billy Roberts

Missy and Billy Roberts had disagreements from the beginning. The marriage was not a good one. Missy was a strong-willed, determined woman. There was something of the earth-mother in her. When she prefaced a response with the word *now*, you knew she meant business and that she wasn't going to give in. My mother, who didn't like her to begin with and thought her "common," was at such times annoyed to distraction. She would hiss through clenched teeth to anyone nearby that there was no way to get through to "that impossible woman!" Billy Roberts, on the other hand, was an uncomplicated fellow, a Customs Agent for the Port of New York. He had no special talents, drive or ambition. He liked his whiskey and his cigars and could be found in his free time loitering in his shirt sleeves with his hands dug deep into his trouser pockets testing the limits of his galluses. The Robertses lived in Jersey for a time. Then Missy met West.

Bernard Westmacott was an Englishman who had emigrated to America around the turn of the century. He was a pen and ink artist who made his living as an illustrator for classic editions of adventure books: Robin Hood, King Arthur, Blackbeard the Pirate. His work closely resembled and paralleled the work of his better-known contemporaries, Howard Pyle and N.C. Wyeth. His father, Richard Westmacott was of the manorial class and had been a sculptor of some note in the waning years of Victoria's reign. Indeed, West (as he preferred to be called) acknowledged with considerable pride that his father had been knighted by the old girl herself thereby becoming Sir Richard Westmacott. (I was often reminded of this brighter footnote to our family history since I was named for him.)

West was well-spoken and well-read having been raised in the Edwardian tradition befitting one of his class. He played cricket and soccer football while attending Oxford. Then, after some serious discussion with his father, he enrolled in art school in London. After traveling on the continent drawing and painting local scenes, he emigrated to America. When war broke out in Europe in 1914, he served with the Canadian army as a sergeant and left a record in a volume of Swinburne's poems that testified that he had been present at Ypres-sur-Marne in 1916.

West was also was a colorful personage, a short wiry man with a brush moustache and an unruly, thick mane of hair. And, he was an inveterate chain smoker. As a child, I marveled as I watched him floating on his back in the waters of Huntington Harbor as he worked a cigarette around in his mouth. I wondered if he smoked in his sleep too and if so, how.

West's insouciance, breeding and old world charm turned Missy's head at once. She had been an artist's model. They met at an exhibit of paintings in a New York apartment-studio. The moment he proposed it and without giving it a second thought, she made off with West leaving both her husband and child behind. The lovers settled in Worcester, Massachussetts for some reason which has escaped the record. They covered their tracks behind them and were not located by the Robertses and the Wittens until Missy returned to pick up some possessions. Angry and indignant, both families merged to force her to take her child back and to assume proper responsibility for him. In the end, Missy divorced Billy Roberts and married West, who had agreed to take a full share in the raising of young Theodore.

Bernard Westmacott

Missy was one of those untroubled people who float carelessly along on the waves of circumstance. She was never bothered by events and their probable consequences. She took things just as they came, and most things none too seriously. Morbid thoughts never entered her mind. The words catastrophe and disaster were not in her lexicon though she'd had her share of them. Her idea was that nothing could be so bad that there wasn't some way to make it better. Her usual reaction was a sing-song, "Oh, that's all right." (My mother gnashed her teeth.) If it was below zero outside and there was no heat inside, she'd put on another sweater, light off the gas stove and put the kettle on for "a good hot cup of tea." If she tripped and fell down an entire flight of stairs, she'd just sit there for a while and laugh and never admit that she was hurt. Missy, too, was slow to anger. But above all, Missy was stubborn.

Missy hated to argue because she knew she'd never back down if it began to look like she was mistaken. The stone plaque imbedded in the wall along Broadway at 204th Street read, "The Dyckman House Park." But the Roman letters were fashioned in 18th century style. The tall s in House looked like an f. To Missy it would ever be "The Dyckman Houfe," *houfe*, of course, being the Dutch word for house. No explanation, however persuasive, however kindly administered by some knowledgeable person could ever convince her otherwise.

Also, she'd quarrel bitterly with her sisters Aunt Anna or Aunt Lil over some trifling detail. It could have been the color of the dress Aunt Clara had worn last Christmas: "Now, Ann, I distinctly remember she had on the green dress, the one with the high neckline."

Aunt Anna would wave her off and croak, "Oh, you don't know what you're talking about. It was that blue velvet she bought years ago in Wanamaker's. Why, you were there when she bought it. You just don't remember, why don't you admit it?"

"Now, Ann, why would you say a thing like that?" Missy would counter indignantly, "I know it was the green dress. She had on her wool hat, the one that matched it." And so it would go between them. Always civil, but with rancor building, Missy held her ground to the last.

If she could abandon her infant son with such wanton disregard and with no thought as to consequences, it's perhaps hard to figure out how she could also be so fiercely loyal and protective of him in later years and then to her grandson. I can remember one instance when I was staying at the Huntington Beach house. West slapped at my hand for picking up food with my fingers. I wahhed off into tears, more from surprise than any physical hurt because West had always passed lightly over my juvenile lapses in decorum. He usually drew my attention to the offense with an animated gesture. He'd make a funny face, an exaggerated expression of distaste. I'd get the message and we'd all laugh and that would be the end of it.

But this was different. Missy and West had been at one another for some time and were squabbling that morning. As it turned out this time, over West's recent sudden and unexplained trips to the City. Missy angered at once: "Now, you just stop it!" she shouted. It was the first time I had ever heard her raise her voice. "You can be angry with me, but don't take it out on the child. You have no right to hit him. You're not his father . . . or even his grandfather for that matter. Tell him what you want him to do, but don't hit him."

It seemed that with any of her progeny, Missy's idea was that young people didn't really ever misbehave. They simply tested the limits of adults' patience. By ignoring them and issuing a cautionary word or two of explanation, children would soon come around and mend their ways.

Regrettably, others didn't always see it that way. Much later in my teen years, Frank Wald, Rudy Gehrmann and I got into a scrape with the police. The trooper who had taken us to the Alpine police barracks phoned the Boathouse and got Missy on the line. When the details had been spelled out Missy erupted: "Breaking in and entry? Dicky? No, you must be mistaken . . . And you say these boys were stealing what? Candy? You arrested them and you're holding them in jail for stealing candy? I never heard of such a thing! . . . Say listen, what is the matter with you people! Now you're treating children like common criminals. Haven't you anything better to do? Now let me tell you something . . . " She did, and I couldn't figure out why the trooper came back to our cage with our supper sandwich redfaced and angry, singling me out: "You, Roberts . . . You better watch your step. I got my eye on you"

6| Boathouse 2

The SC 81 off Corfu Island

MY FATHER HAD served in the Navy on a subchaser, the SC 81 of the "Splinter Fleet" during the World War we entered in 1917. After an additional year in the merchant service, he decided to go into the boat business for himself. West advanced him most of the money needed to buy Smith's Boathouse, and they both worked on enlarging the place. They added a long, boat storage shed on the south side of the main house and another, larger float with two gangways. On the north side they put up a locker room extending the decking around it. The additional deck space made possible the addition of a chain hoist and outdoor dock space where larger, outboard motor boats could be stored during the winter months.

To help them with the construction, West and my father hired a handyman. They built a tiny, two-room shed for him to live in, adjoining the locker room. Inside, they put a cot, a stove, a table and a chest of drawers. Some years later, after the upper story of the Boathouse was renovated to become a year-round dwelling, Missy occupied this same shed when she stayed over to help my father. When we as a family moved into the Boathouse, I came to know the little shed as "Missy's house."

The expanded structure was now called West's Boathouse, and it continued to be the home of the old Spuyten Duyvil Boat & Canoe Club. I remember vividly the logo for the Club. It excited my imagination as a child. In a circle there was the silhouette of a devil holding a canoe paddle over one shoulder while he beckoned with the other arm. His tail was unusually long. It looped around the paddle and ended as the flukes of an anchor.

As noted earlier, the "devil" idea in Spuyten Duyvil was the result of a common mistranslation of the Old Dutch name for the original creek that separated the northern extremity of Manhattan Island from the mainland. (One British Revolutionary War map made it out "Spiting Devil.") But it was Washington Irving's legend in the *Knickerbocker History of New York* that left us with the definitive misnomer. It seems that Anthony van Corlear, Peter Stuyvesant's faithful squire and trumpeter was sent by Stuyvesant to rouse the villagers in the Hudson Valley letting them know that the Yankee English were coming. Van Corlear had to swim the Creek in a raging storm "Spyt den Duyvel" or, In Spite of the Devil as Irving interpreted it. The "Devil," in this case, was a great fish that swallowed him up, but not before he was able to give out with one long, resounding blast on his trumpet which was heard forevermore in the surrounding hillsides whenever there was a storm. Van Corlear is memorialized by a street named for him near the site in the Marble Hill section.

But the far less colorful, though evidently correct translation of Spuyten Duyvel (later, Duyvil) is "spouting meadow," The name refers to the spring which ran down from Inwood Hill Park into the flats that bordered the Creek. The area, in fact, at one time was known as Cold Spring.

I mentioned that the upper story of the Boathouse had been laid out in rough fashion with living quarters. At the time it was built, electric power lines had not yet been run in. Gas jets poked out of the walls here and there in each room of the crude apartment. The old Inwood gas storage tank some small distance above the five-corners intersection between Dyckman Street, Broadway and Riverside Drive provided the means for every needed energy source—gas for light, heat, and for cooking. And, while a city water line had been run in, the river served as a sewer.

Temporarily, my father and West occupied the original quarters while they worked on the additions to the house. West split his time between the Boathouse and his apartment on 14th Street where he and Missy lived. Then, when the additions to the Boathouse were completed, my father, now married, rented an apartment nearby on Academy and Cooper Street for his bride and himself.

7| Missy 2

MY EARLIEST RECOLLECTIONS of the Boathouse were associated with Missy. She often came up from 14th Street to help out, mainly to direct traffic and sell soda pop from behind the counter and answer questions for boat or canoe owner tenants.

When Missy was at the boathouse, everyone knew it. She was a distinct presence, beginning most likely with the way she looked. In the warm months she'd wear a dark, one-color organdy dress. The dress would have a prominent collar and oftentimes a frilly jabot. On her head she always wore a wide-brimmed straw or floppy cotton hat with a faded ribbon band (a "Missy hat"). She might accent this ensemble with a long string of yellow agate beads. And, she was never without her pince-nez glasses which dangled from her neck onto her ample bosom by a narrow black ribbon.

Missy would station herself in her favorite chair by the heavy pocket doors of the main house that met in the center when closed, and when open, looked out onto the river. Here was a good vantage point. Missy had time to watch as intruders came down the ramp from the road and entered the Boathouse. They made their way through the main house to where she sat sentinel on the dock in the sun. Squinting down the alleyway, she was ready at a moment's notice to challenge an unfamiliar figure, perhaps someone who had innocently strolled in to take in the scene. "Can I help you?" She seemed to sense that he was a loafer up to no good. The answer was usually a faltering variation of no. Missy was ready for it: "This is a private club for tenants and their families and guests. Do you have someone here?" Again, no. "Then I'm afraid you'll have to leave. There's a public dock by the ferry slip." The interloper, intimidated, would choke out a word or two of apology and drift out as casually as he drifted in.

Missy Sitting Sentinel

Missy was effective with tenants too. If a tenant even momentarily moved a boat into a place that restricted passage while he stopped to hail a friend coming up a gangway she'd waken into action. "Say, Mr. Schwerner, you can't leave that boat there like that. Other tenants have to get by and they can't." Her voice had the cutting edge of authority. Mr. Schwerner moved the boat and the matter was corrected without further ado.

In fact Missy was often a busy, imperious and tactless woman who nosed around the Boathouse collaring tenants by name, pressing them for information about their families and prying into their personal lives and business as though it were her sovereign duty to keep track of such things. "Oh? Mrs. Molloy isn't with you today? Isn't she well? She isn't still afraid of the canoe tipping over, is she? You know what you ought to try? . . . Let her go out by herself some time . . . Don't tell her. Just settle her into the bottom of the canoe with a paddle and push her off from the float."

8| Locale 1

THE INWOOD I knew as a boy in the late 1920s and 1930s was that narrow, bone-shaped northern tip of Manhattan Island that fitted neatly into the socket of the Bronx. As a part of the thirteen-mile length of the Island, and being perfectly contained within its shores, Inwood belongs to the City and County of New York. It always irked me when people referred to it as the Bronx. "It's *not* the Bronx," I'd say. "You know where Washington Heights is? . . . Fort Tryon Park, the Cloisters? . . . Okay, it's just up from there." I'd point a finger northwards, hoping to clarify the geography. I wanted to dispel any notion that Inwood was any part of the alien and inferior Bronx. The listener would squint uncertainly. He never knew there was anything "up from there."

Then, as now, Inwood is indisputably a part of Manhattan Island. It is bounded on the west by the Hudson River and on the east by the Harlem River, and on the north by Spuyten Duyvil Creek. The original Creek, as it meandered inland from the Hudson became at one point a shallow, fordable stream at low tides. Later, its limitations as a navigable waterway were removed by the construction of the Harlem River Ship Canal in 1895 which made passage between the two larger waterways possible. In fact, the Canal actually cut off a part of the original Island, the little knob called Marble Hill that now looks on land maps like a part of the Bronx mainland. Political boundaries still show Marble Hill as being in New York County and not Bronx County.

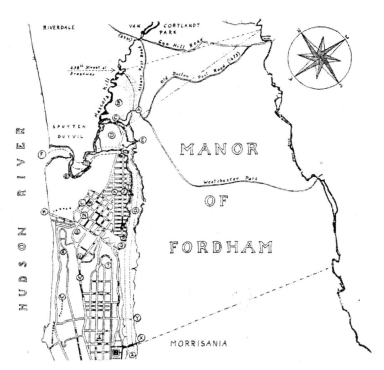

NORTHERN MANHATTAN & MANOR OF FORDHAM

A Fordham Village
B Papariniman Island
C The King's Bridge
D Marble Hill
E Dyckman's (Farmers') Bridge
F Spuyten Duyvil Creek
G Indian Cave
H Tubby Hook Landing
I Nagel's (Century) House
J Nagel Burying Ground
K Slave Burying Ground
L British Hut Camp
M Dyckman House

N Public School No. 52
O Footbridge to Fordham
P Bronson's Point
Q Sherman's Bay
R Fort Tryon
S Body Regiment
T Fort George
U Sowerby House
V Barrier Gate
W Fort Washington
X High Bridge
Y Washington Bridge
Z Harlem River*

* Dotted lines mark present Harlem banks and channel of Ship Canal.

The southern, or city-side boundary of Inwood is harder to establish. I always used to think of it as Dyckman Street because of the wide, store-lined boulevard that crossed the Island obliquely from river to river. My feeling was, once you climbed the hills of Fort George or Fort Tryon; or followed the Broadway streetcar tracks as they worked their way uphill from Dyckman Street, you had left Inwood behind for Washington Heights and the City proper. As it turns out, I wasn't entirely wrong.

In reality, a small part of Inwood does run south from Dyckman Street. This small, seemingly separate part of the Vale of Inwood is enclosed within a loop that begins at Dyckman Street and Broadway, runs south along Broadway to Hillside Avenue, then turns to the east and goes back to Dyckman Street where Nagle Avenue and Fort George Hill intersect, and where there is a subway (actually, elevated) stop. These twenty odd acres were once called the Ronde Vlys, open fields deeded to the Flemish Kortright brothers in 1691. By the 1920s this area was scored by city blocks that extended the Inwood grid, and these were afterwards filled in mainly with five and six-story apartment buildings. To my way of thinking these uninteresting alleyways were just shadowy passageways to better places.

Early maps not only help to explain the course of Dyckman Street, but also serve to define the natural boundaries of Inwood which set it apart from the rest of the City. At one time an inlet from the Harlem River cut deeply into the land separating the heights of Fort George from the Round Meadow or Muscoota flatlands to the north where the old car barns and subway yards were built. The Half-Creek, renamed Sherman's Bay for the family that lived on its banks in the early 1800s had a number of tributaries. They issued from the cut as tiny streams. One such stream, called Pieter Tuynier's Run flowed well inland along the valley floor that crossed the Island between the western elevations of Fort Tryon Park and Inwood Hill Park. Tuynier's Run almost certainly determined the course of the Dyckman Street of today.

In fact, it is not hard to imagine that at an earlier geological time Inwood was an island in its own right. And if this were the case, the Broadway-Hillside, Ronde Vlys loop would have been cut off. If I'd known about that at the time, I might have been able to support my argument that this bowl between the hills was not originally a part of Inwood.

9| Claude & Marjorie

MY MOTHER MET Evelyn Rolland and Sally Quinn along Payson Avenue when Claude and Marjorie and I were still infants in carriages. We were living in the apartment at Academy and Cumming Street at the time, and on a sunny, summer afternoon, Mother got into the habit of settling me into the carriage and walking over to the shade trees of Payson Avenue bordering Inwood Hill Park to look for her new friends. She discovered that it was agreeable to meet them at this time of day and to share the experiences and concerns that most young mothers have as they strolled up Bolton Road into the sylvan recesses of Inwood Hill Park—if time permitted, as far as the McCreery mansion. When we grew out of our baby carriages our mothers continued their pleasant relationship.

By the time we had moved to 2 Seaman Avenue both the Rollands and the Quinns had moved away from Inwood. The Rollands had bought a two story frame house in New Rochelle while the Quinns, crowned by the success of Ed Quinn's Chevrolet dealership in Manhattan, moved into a Tudor style home in fashionable Hastings-on-the-Hudson. The mothers phoned and visited with one another regularly. Soon Claude, Marjorie and I were old enough to look forward to these visits as a special afternoon of play.

I have it on my mother's good authority that Marjorie was a tease by the time she was three years old. On one of those visits when mothers and children got together Marjorie had been sucking on a lolly pop. She held it out to me, "Here, want a lick?" Then she pulled it back. I had been playing in the sand with a toy pail and shovel. She did this three times before I cracked her over the skull with the shovel. As the story goes, it took three stitches to stop the bleeding. Happily, the incident was understood by the mothers in its proper perspective, and Marjorie and I continued to see one another as we advanced from one birthday party to the next.

Claude, as soon as he could run, developed a quirk that he carried even on into his teen years. Evelyn had an unusually powerful voice, one that both carried and penetrated right to the core of the listener's being . I don't think that Claude was perverse by nature, but when he heard his mother's strident call, "Claw-ud!" for him to come, instead of coming, he ran away. He'd never be far off. He'd pick a place to hide where he could peek out and watch and not be seen. He'd follow along, darting from this corner to the next, and the more Evelyn hollered the longer he stayed hidden. Of course he came back sooner or later, once it was quiet.

I looked on Claude's running off as a family matter and stayed out of it. Nor did I ever ask him why he did it. I knew I'd never get an answer. (But I do have to admit that I watched each episode with a certain smug amusement.) What was more important to me was that Claude and I complemented one another very well in the imagination sector. We dreamed up a wealth of Huck Finn adventures and we shared many confidences over the years.

As I became more boy and Marjorie became more girl, we saw less of one another. It was safe for me to think of her as a girlfriend because of the distance we lived from one another, and because our intimacy was tied to our early side-by-side association as infant neuters. But as we grew older, it was usually only the birthday of one or the other that brought us together. I have to add that our birthday parties were always pleasant and happily-remembered events from year to year. Under these circumstances, it was possible for boys and girls to play little games with one another and to find things we liked about one another. On the other hand, I had already begun to believe that the real intimacies and pleasures of growing up were to be found only among boys.

10| Ole 1

OLAF SWENSEN MUST have been about four years old when I discovered him. It was in the open courtyard to the apartment building at 2-12 Seaman Avenue. We had recently moved into a more spacious apartment in this building from the one at Cooper and Academy Streets. Ole was the super's kid in the new building. He lived in the cellar apartment with his family. I knew his name before I knew him. His mother, while no Swedish Nightingale, fairly sang for him to come: "O-lee!" The call echoed up the air shafts of the building.

This new apartment building, obliquely across from the old Mount Washington Valley Church, had awakened Inwood's denizens to the pre-history of their community even before its foundation had been laid. Steam-shoveling into the boggy subsoil, workers unearthed a great, curling mammoth tusk in an excellent state of preservation. The find was authenticated by paleontologists and was promptly shipped off to the American Museum of Natural History for further study, classification and display.

Unfortunately, no sooner had the five-story building gone up than it began to settle into the mire. Had it not been for its twin, 1-49 Payson Avenue, built first, the structure would probably have sunk off to an unacceptable angle. But as it was, the two buildings leaned against and buttressed one another along Dyckman Street from Seaman Avenue to Payson Avenue, the one lower than the other. They remain that way today.

Ole Swensen was a frail child at four with a great mop of golden curls which his mother refused to cut until he went to school, in keeping with the customs of an earlier time and place. Ole's head glowed like a beacon radiating his tender years and frail being. It set him apart instantly from other children, and it was what you looked for when you looked for Ole.

But Ole had other marks that distinguished him. He was he was scarred very early in life. The exact details were never really clear to me, but even before I knew him, Ole's face had been slashed along the right eye. The wound had apparently been made from a piece of window glass hurtling down into the cellar well where he was playing one day. The jagged scar ran from his temple to his cheekbone marking him for life. Then in a series of accidents resulting from falls taken while running in Inwood Hill Park, he managed breaks in both of his legs, and in one of his arms by the time he was seven.

Both of Ole's parents were Scandinavian. His father, the super, was a watery-eyed Dane who had a kinship with alcohol. His mother was a heavy-set, mournful Swede. At the time I found him, Ole had one older sister, Ingrid by name and a fresh kid by nature. Mother and father spoke English to one another, but not without some of the characteristic difficulties Scandinavians have with the English language. As a result, Ole learned to say "yoost" for *just*, and "aw-vus" for *always*. These mispronunciations rubbed off quickly on me as I got to know Ole better, and I took them home with me. My mother and father laughed and told me how the words ought to be said. It was my introduction to the idea that there was a right way and a wrong way to talk.

I always think of Ole as the one kid I knew uninterrupted from pre-school years to beyond our discharge from the armed forces. I think of him too as the first friend that I made on my own and not one that was made for me. While our mothers must have exchanged words on the matter of child rearing, Ole and I were never put together and told to go off and play. We simply met up with one another in the courtyard of the apartment building and began to play some little game. From then on, it was easy to find things to do. We discovered that we both had vivid imaginations and delighted in working them to full advantage while we played together. We found, like most children, that we could quickly create and live in a world of our own making, a world full of action and adventure where we were always the good guys who won out in the end. It was inevitable that we would select the apartment building as our first playground—in fact, we had no choice in the matter; we were limited to it.

For us, 2-12 Seaman Avenue was a great castle, a marvelous structure to explore where we found stairs to climb and hidden recesses. The building had a large courtyard with sculpted lions at the sidewalk entrance. Double doors led to a foyer inside where there were hallways to either side At the ends there were dark alcoves with rows of mailboxes—good places to hide. There were stairs to either side with turns at each landing. There were five flights with tiled hallways at each landing and strong looking doors to apartments. Then came that final sky-lit stairway up to the heavy, sheet metal covered door that opened out onto the flat, tar-papered roof with its vents, clothes lines, and radio antennas. From over the tile caps at the roof's edge, the world below looked small. The smell of the tar in the hot sun mingled with the smell of the wet wash hung out to dry.

Ole and I were barons in this great castle. In improvised play that grew in dimension and complexity from moment to moment and day to day, we darted out of the dungeon-like cellar by Ole's apartment door and climbed the apartment stairs from landing to landing. Now it was a dragon that lunged out from around a corner; then it was an army of renegade knights who rushed at us from the corridors past the apartment doors and engaged us in heated combat. Holding our own, we fought our way up to the top landing and forced our way out through the great door into the sunlight and out onto the parapet where we clashed with the opposing army. At last the battle was over; we had triumphed. The renegade knights had been defeated. We had won the day. We were fulfilled and happy.

11| Babyface

IT WAS OPPRESSIVELY hot in our apartment at 2 Seaman during that summer of 1929. The air just didn't want to move. To make matters worse, I had caught whooping cough from Ole. Dr. Price advised my mother to get me out of the city if she could. He said that I needed to be where I could breathe easier, where there would be fresh air.

Grandpa and Grandma Freudiger lived in an old, cedar shingled house on the edge of the small town of Lincoln Park, New Jersey. It was about twenty-five miles from the City. The air was good there. There was always a breeze from the nearby hills.

My father agreed that my mother should take the Buick and drive me out to Lincoln Park. She would stay out there with me until I was better. My father would live at the Boathouse for the time being. It would save him from walking back and forth to the apartment since it was the height of the boating season. It was arranged, too, that Missy West should come up from 14th Street to stay at the Boathouse to do the cooking and household chores.

In 1929 the manufacture and sale of alcoholic beverages was prohibited by law. In 1919, Congress had overridden the President's veto and passed the 18th Amendment which a year later was enforced by the Volstead Act. America went dry for thirteen years. Almost immediately a vast, illegal liquor trade had filled the gap.

By now it had become well-established and was flourishing. Rum-runners, bootleggers and gangsters vied for control and operated within plain sight of the law in every community of any consequence across the country. This new entrepreneurial class smuggled booze past the authorities and into sinister dens called speakeasies. As it happened, just such a place had crept into a corner of the old church parish house (by then Charley Veitch's garage) across Dyckman Street from our apartment.

One night a blast rattled our windows. The speakeasy had been bombed out. But within a week a new gin mill had moved into a storefront on our side of the street, as a matter of fact, directly under our kitchen window. When the stock market tumbled toward the end of the year followed by the bank failures, Mother used her knowledge of the speakeasy menace to break our lease at 2 Seaman. But that's another story.

Readying for the drive to Jersey, my mother settled me into the back seat of the Buick. Exhausted from whooping, I fell asleep at once while she loaded the valises into the trunk of the car. At last she settled into the driver's seat and found the starter button with her foot.

She coaxed the engine with the accelerator and put the car into gear and rolled down the ramp of Veitch's garage. She pulled into line along Dyckman Street with the other cars waiting for the ferry. The sun beat down on the belgian block cobblestones melting the tar between them. The air was muggy and still. Waiting motorists got out of their cars, mopped their brows with handkerchiefs and headed for the soda pop stands.

After what seemed an eternity, Mother followed the ferry deckhand's signals and found the lane he pointed to. She eased to a stop in the inboard lane of the right alley of the ferryboat. She noticed that she was alongside the open door to the engine well. She watched as the massive crankshaft of the old walking beam steam engine began its great arc, swinging slowly upward from the bilges of the boat splashing the sidewheels against the water outside of the hull. The thick smell of steam and grease drifted into the car. Mother felt a wave of nausea and thought about getting out of the car and walking to the front of the boat.

But then she remembered me on the back seat. The boat would be moving out of the slip soon and into the river. The air would move. She never noticed the slender young man with the roadmap in his hand who had sidled up to her car window along the narrow ledge between the cars and the bulkhead.

"Excuse me, ma'am." Mother jumped, then became aware of the speaker. He was a well-groomed young man in a dark double-breasted suit with a bow tie. He wore a grey fedora hat. He could have been in his early twenties, or even in his late teens. She took particular notice of his round, boyish face.

"Sorry, ma'am. I didn't mean to startle you," he said and presented the folded map. "We want to get to Phillipsburg. Here . . ." he pointed. "We're looking for the best roads . . . Do you know anything about the roads?"

Having made the trip to Lincoln Park many times before, my mother had got to know the roads well, especially the back roads which were less traveled and saved time. She recalled the road sign on the Pompton Pike pointing the way to Easton, Allentown and Phillipsburg. "If you want to follow me, I can take you to where you turn off." She studied the boyish face.

"Sure thing," said the boy-face.

"But, I go by the back roads," warned Mother. "A lot of turns, but quicker."

"That's jake with us," grinned the boy-face "We'll be right behind you," he assured.

Mother watched the young man make his way back to his car through her rear-view window. The car was directly behind hers, a black touring car. It looked new. She noticed that there were three other men in it, all as young as boy-face.

The ferry grazed the pilings of the slip on the Jersey shore making them groan. The ferry's rounded nose made its way into the crescent. Then a clanking chain hoist lowered a ramp to meet it. Car engines roared to life one after another.

Mother followed the procession, winding up the hairpin turns of the Palisades to Englewood. She got to Palisades Avenue and saw that the sky had suddenly blackened. She could hear the thunder echoing in the distance. At the outskirts of Teaneck she turned off onto a road that ran south along the Hackensack River. The rain began to fall, a few heavy drops at first, then in torrents. The Buick's windshield wipers were all but useless. Mother shifted down and rolled along slowly, every now and then spotting patches of grass showing where the side of the road was. She had forgot completely about the black touring car behind her. Her eyes were riveted on the road.

The rain eased up some as Mother crossed the Passaic River and snaked her way through Paterson. But the air remained heavy and it was just as sultry as it had been before the storm.

Outside Paterson, Mother climbed a hill along Union Avenue and noticed that the engine was laboring. She read the gauge on the dashboard. The needle rested just below the 200 mark. Mother could smell the alcohol-laced vapor escaping from the radiator. She barely made it to the station at the Singac crossroads.

She turned off the engine and got out of the car alongside the pumps. The touring car with its four youthful occupants swept up alongside her and jerked to a stop. Boy-face leaped out and ran over to where Mother stood by the engine hood of her car. He grabbed her by the arm, his eyes fixed on her, scanning her face. "Say, listen, lady. What're you trying to pull?" he said.

"I'm not trying to pull anything," said Mother. "Let go of my arm." She shook loose of his grip. "I'd like to take care of my car," she nodded in the direction of the wounded vehicle. "That is, if you don't mind."

Boy-face became aware of the hiss of the cooking engine and the tainted fumes. Before he could react Mother said, "I offered, very nicely I think, to take you to where you could get the Phillipsburg Road," she pointed at the intersecting roads. "That's the signpost over there." Boyface turned his head and squinted. "You can read, can't you?" added Mother sensing an opportunity to get even for an injury. "So why don't you just be on your way and let me take care of my car."

The hard look on the young man's face softened into a grin. "No offence, maam. We nearly lost you in all that rain back there. Made me a little jumpy, I guess. And say . . . Thanks for the help." He inched his way back to his car and his companions. He had left his engine running. He put the car in gear now, waved and drove off.

The Buick's engine had cooled down. The station attendant asked Mother to start the engine. He added water to the radiator from the galvanized can with the long spout. A few minutes later Mother was on her way once again.

My whooping cough ran its course and we stayed in Lincoln Park for almost two weeks, until the worst of the heatwave had passed. We were no sooner back in our apartment in Inwood than the doorbell rang. It was Mrs. Martinelli from next door. She was excited and clutched a tabloid in her hand. "You heard about the shooting?" she said to my mother.

"Shooting? What shooting?" asked Mother.

"It was in all the papers. You didn't see? In the speakeasy downstairs there was a gang war while you were away. Your husband didn't tell you?"

"He didn't tell me anything about any gang wars." said Mother.

"Here . . . Look here." Mrs. Martinelli spread the newspaper out on the kitchen table. "It was something, I can tell you. Police, fire engines, ambulances . . ."

Mother looked at the photographs that went with the story in the New York daily. She grabbbed the paper to have a closer look, "My God, that's him!"

"Him? Who 'him'?" Mrs. Martinelli questioned.

Mother told her about the man on the ferry who had asked her for directions to Phillipsburg and how she led him partway until her car gave out and how he accosted her.

"That's him!" she pointed at the pictures. "That's the guy!"

"Ooh," exclaimed Mrs. Martinelli, her eyes opening wide, "That's the one that was killed!"

Mother began to read. The papers called him a "baby-faced

killer." He and the others with him were suspected of having slaughtered several rival gang members and a couple of innocent people in the Bronx in a similar style gun battle a few weeks ago. They had escaped and made their way to Pennsylvania where they hid out for a time and then returned to New York to resume their activities. The federal authorities had posted a description of the men which carried a photograph of the young public enemy, lately-deceased.

Mother looked up at the calendar on the wall. She had circled the date we left for Lincoln Park. She reread the newspaper story locating the date of the Bronx massacre. Sure enough, it was the same day.

That night Mother was quick to ask my father why he didn't tell her about the shootings downstairs when he phoned. My father said he didn't want to alarm her. Then she told him about what had happened.

"Are you sure it was him?" said my father. "The same guy, I mean."

"Am I sure?" She pushed the newspaper at my father. "What do you think? I wouldn't remember some maniac who grabs me out of the blue for no reason at all? I wouldn't remember his face?"

My father sighed and was silent for a moment. "How many people have you told about this?" he asked finally.

"Nobody," said Mother. "I haven't had a chance to tell anybody . . . Well, Mrs. Martinelli. But if she hadn't shown me the paper, I wouldn't have known about it myself."

"Well, don't tell anybody," said Father. "There were other men, you said. They saw you and they saw your car. If any of them were mixed up in that business downstairs and got away, it might not be so good."

Mother took the warning to heart. Her lips were sealed for some time to come. Neither she nor the car went out very much.

By the time it was agreed that it was safe for my mother to tell the story of her adventure with the underworld, the story had gathered the trappings of a classic tale:

"Dickie had this terrible case of whooping cough. He could hardly breathe. The doctor said I had to get him to the country or he could die. Somehow I knew even before I got on the ferry, I was being watched. Then I drove with these awful men behind me through the worst thunderstorm I ever saw. It was a miracle I got through it in one piece. And there, right behind me all the time, was that huge black car. Of course, I didn't know it at the time, but it was Baby Face Nelson and his gang! Imagine, this young man who was so polite on the ferry. He was a killer! A fugitive . . . He grabbed me and held onto me. He could have killed me without blinking an eye. And there was Dickie on the back seat of the car. He slept through it all."

Mother in the Buick in 1929

Unfortunately, there is still some question as to who the central figure of Mother's story actually was, even if the other details suffered only from exaggeration. And while there is no reason to doubt that the man in the photograph who was killed and the man who accosted her were one in the same, he could not have been Baby Face Nelson. Nelson was killed by G-men in Illinois in 1934.

I was never able to find any record of the gunbattle fought in the Dyckman Street speakeasy. And there was no one around who remembered the incident or the boy-face menace.

12| Boathouse 3

WHEN OUR SMALL family moved from Academy Street two blocks or so away to a newer, more spacious apartment at 2 Seaman Avenue my father had an even shorter walk to his place of business, the Boathouse. Like any other businessman, he left for work in the morning and returned to the apartment in the evening. It was at the time before West had bought the Huntington Beach house, and Missy or West was able to stay on at the Boathouse during the busy boating season. My father could then spend the evening at the apartment with his family. The arrangement, if it was not always easy for my father to work out, was agreeable for my mother. She had the stores nearby and the whole of Inwood Hill Park to roam around in with the other young mothers she had met. And, as an additional bonus, she didn't have Missy to contend with.

Unfortunately, but necessarily, within the space of a few years things had to change. Following the economic crises of the first years of the thirties during which we lost all of our savings in the Bank of America, we were forced to give up the apartment at 2 Seaman Avenue. I had already begun kindergarten at P.S. 52 when my father decided that my mother and I should move out to Lincoln Park for the time being and live with Grandpa and Grandma Freudiger. With the boating season coming on, my father would have to stay in Inwood and live at the Boathouse and visit us when he could. Then as the season slackened in late summer he could begin to remodel the rude living quarters, making them fit for winter habitation. If all went well we would return to make our home at the Boathouse in the fall.

Misfortunes as they say have a way of compounding themselves. Grandma Freudiger died that summer. This put an additional burden on my mother as we lived on in New Jersey. In September I was enrolled in the small Lincoln Park school, while back at the Boathouse my father continued his work on the upstairs level of the main house. After an electrical contractor had put in wiring, my father added insulation to the attic and walls, replacing the old wainscoting with plywood wall paneling. He installed a modern coal burning stove in the living room, put a hot water tank and refrigerator in the kitchen and added new plumbing to both kitchen and bathroom. The place was now livable as a year-round residence for a small family.

Missy spent most of her time at the Boathouse that year of the refurbishing. West would show up when he could from the 14th Street apartment to help out. Missy kept house and did the cooking for the men, first from the little shed off the locker room where she slept; then later from upstairs in the main house where she moved when the rooms were completed. My father was able to make weekly trips to Lincoln Park to spend time with my mother and me. At last, in the fall of 1931, the living quarters were ready and we were united once again as a family.

On our return to Inwood, Missy and West took up their lives once again in their small, 14th Street basement apartment. Except for occasional visits, Missy and West left the Boathouse entirely to us. Some years later, and with West's blessing, the sign on the Boathouse looking out on the river reading: "West's" was taken down and a new one put up. The new sign read: "T. Roberts."

Late in that troubled year of 1931, I was enrolled in the 1st Grade at P.S. 52, Manhattan. The imposing five-story red brick and stone structure, with its castle-like main entrance on Academy Street, cornered at Vermilyea Avenue. Completed in 1920 to accommodate the growing population of Inwood, it replaced the original three-story building at the Broadway end of Academy Street that had served the community since 1857. Now between the Boathouse and school my life attached itself to a round of yearly events that varied little for almost ten years.

13| Institutions

THE INSTITUTIONS OF a community determine the quality of life for those who live there. The community, as implied earlier, takes on a life of its own. It receives and upholds the living standards that are passed along to it, and it changes them to be in harmony with the times. These social values in turn are accepted as institutions that govern the way the current generation will live.

Institutions are the tapestries of life. They are places to go to and things to do. They are people: a mother and a father, brothers, sisters, a grandmother, friends, teachers. They are the seasons: Christmas, Easter and Passover, Decoration Day, the Fourth of July, summer and fall. They are the means of transportation: automobiles, trolleys, buses and subways. They are familiar buildings: apartments, private homes, schools; ballfields, skating rinks, swimming pools, and parks. They are the things we agree to do together. Institutions then, are the accepted ways of communal life. And they will vary in a place, as implied, according to the times.

We, the children of the Inwood of the late 20s and 1930s, grew to adulthood at a unique time. Our institutions were abridged by an ongoing economic depression that forced us consistently to get a lot out of a little. There was the father who had to give up an apartment and add living quarters to his place of business for his family; the mother whose husband died suddenly leaving her with two small children, and who had to move to a cheaper apartment and find work quickly, counting on her children to care for themselves; the brother who had to quit school in the ninth grade to work full-time to help support the family; the super's kid who was thrilled to go for a ride in an automobile; the afternoon baseball game with rocks for bases and a hideless, black friction-taped baseball; slipping under a subway turnstile to go to the Museum of Natural History; Saturday afternoons at the movies for ten cents where the next chapter of Flash Gordon or Fu Man Chu was playing; nickel ferryboat rides to Jersey and back; roller skate street-hockey games with chalked out goals and a square of wood for a puck; match fights—gripping the wooden match, thumbnail at the head, ready, waiting for the right moment to scratch and fling the lighted match at a circling opponent; ten cent "Big-little Books"—page after page of a Dick Tracy adventure; a chill morning lift to school with the milkman in his horse-drawn cart; a trombone with a jammed slide a friend sold me for fifty-cents; miniature balsa wood World War airplane kits from which I cut, shaped, sanded, glued and painted a Fokker D-VII or a Spad, that I hung from my bedroom ceiling with fine black threads; a nickel bet that I wouldn't kiss the little blond girl who stood by the playground watching us play ball every afternoon; and, the spring treks through Inwood Hill Park where we looked for arrowheads, poked at skunk cabbage and collected jack-in-the pulpits near the Great Tulip Tree.

There were those familiar stamping grounds: the Payson Avenue playground and Park House; P.S. 52 and JHS 52's Great School Yard; Irv's newspaper stand and candy store; the IND Subway stop at Broadway and Dyckman Street; further along, Woolworth's and Kresge's five-and-ten cent stores; the Speedway along the Harlem River and the warm weather "carnies;" the Polo Grounds, home of the New York Giants baseball club; the sand lot ball fields at Farmer's Field; the playground at Isham Street with its monkey bars and World War cannon; Fort Tryon Park and the Cloisters; Loew's Inwood and the Alpine movie theaters; the Miramar Salt Water Swimming Pool; the Dyckman

Oval and the Hamilton Tennis Courts and Ice Skating Rink; Mount Washington Presbyterian Church with its Sunday school rooms and basketball court; and always, Inwood Hill Park with its potholes and caves.

In these varied precincts we spent winter afternoons after school throwing rocks at the remaining panes of the old Inwood School at Broadway and Academy Street, or played King of the Hill on mounds of dirty snow plowed high, or torched dry Christmas trees at the curbstones of Academy Street. In P.S. 52, Manhattan we pored over the school's library books for pictures and stories of enchanted lands and people: Greek heroes and Norse gods, extinct reptilian monsters, the great palms of Tahiti; and buried treasure. We discovered Blind Pew, Odysseus and Thor; the brontosaur in Wells's *Outline of History*. On rainy afternoons, in one or the other's apartments, we sifted through postage stamps and looked for the right printed square in the Scott stamp album to hinge them in—we counted our change so that we could buy commemorative issues at the post office on Vermilyea Avenue. Sometimes we flipped baseball, movie star or gangster cards; we painted bright colors on lead soldiers with strong-smelling paint, or created perfect geometric designs with a compass while propped up in bed getting over the measles. At other times we climbed over the rocks in Inwood Hill Park or built fires to roast mickeys on a cold autumn afternoon. In our homes we listened to our favorite fifteen-minute radio shows: Uncle Don, The Singing Lady, Orphan Annie, Jack Armstrong. Waiting for the school's afternoon session bell, we watched the Great Schoolyard fist-fights—crowds of kids circling their battling friends cheering them on. From Inwood we took the Broadway street car to chunky Doctor Price's office and his antiseptic-smelling examining room in his apartment building up on Washington Heights, the one with the diamond light windows by 180th Street; or, we took the subway to the Bronx, to Shapiro's apartment, the family dentist who told you to "open wide, just a little more . . ." At the Boathouse, I might bring a schoolfriend, and we would climb into the dirty attic to run the Lionel trains after dusting off the three-rail tracks; or, maybe take the skiff at low tide and pole around the cribs under the house; and year by year grow taller observing the familiar Boathouse tenants—half-blind Olivella and his pasty-faced and painfully shy, yellow-haired wife who could barely manage a hello, a yes, a no; or O'Connell, the skinny, ever-smiling, good-natured drunk who always wore a grey fedora hat and a black overcoat over his carefully tailored pin stripe suit, and who bathed you in alcohol fumes whenever he talked; or Sponse (he had a Sponson boat) who was most times called Flipper Feet because he had wide, flat feet—a good-natured guy whose real name nobody ever knew.

There were our legendary heroes too: Joe Louis, the New York Giants or Yankees or Brooklyn Dodgers, and the ever-President, Franklin D. Roosevelt. There were quickly improvised games: one o'cat, box ball, hit-the-point or kick the-can, hide-and seek or ring-a-lee-vee-o in Inwood Hill Park. Then there were the immense urinals in the disinfectant-smelling Boys Room on the ground level of P.S. 52. There was dressing for school: always a shirt and a tie (white and red for Friday assembly days) and knickers till you were thirteen; and homework with never-ending arithmetic examples and problems. There were family Friday nights out: a spaghetti dinner and a movie at Loew's 175th Street where they gave away free dishes or played Screeno, or the Coliseum where they featured vaudeville with the movie. There were those first days at summer camp trying to ward off homesickness by burning the outlines of pictures on a piece of wood. There were birthday parties with paper hats and snappers, school promotions and graduations rewarded by a quarter and a treat to the show at Radio City Music Hall. In all, a complex blend of the basic ingredients of living—varied, unlimited, and wholly satisfying.

14| Locale 2

AS I NOTED earlier, my first awareness of Inwood began with our three-room apartment at 2 Seaman Avenue which overlooked Seaman Avenue and the wide, belgian block cobble-stoned roadway of Dyckman Street below my bedroom window. From this window I could look up toward Broadway and see the old Valley Church with its prominent spire. The church, about to be torn down to make way for street improvements, was originally called the Mount Washington Valley Church. The slender wooden structure stood in the triangle made by the intersection of Broadway, Dyckman Street and Riverside Drive. Immediately across from my window was the Church's parish house, built in 1914. The stone building had already been converted into Ralph Oakley's marine hardware store and adjoined Charley Veitch's garage. The church itself moved into its new street front building at 84 Vermilyea Avenue in 1929.

There was always traffic on Dyckman Street, even at our sparsely populated end due to the ferry that crossed the Hudson to New Jersey and Englewood Cliffs before the George Washington Bridge was completed in 1931. Two old, wooden side-wheel steamers with names emblazoned in great gold letters like the GEORGE W. PERKINS on their sides cris-crossed the River at twenty minute intervals. Cars and trucks lined up along Dyckman Street under the castle-like, brownstone of the first Jewish Memorial Hospital waiting to enter the slip. There were a handful of rickety stands on either side of the street where vendors with

Mediterranean accents tempted waiting motorists with colored soda water, candy bars, Eskimo Pies and Dixie Cups. This was legitimate loafing time, and drivers and passengers lolled around eating, drinking, smoking and chatting with one another while they waited for the next ferry. Life was a good deal slower then.

This ferry-end of Dyckman Street from the Hudson River to Broadway (or the Kings Bridge Road, as it was known some time earlier) had originally been called Inwood Street and was associated with old Tubby Hook and the Valley Church that served it.

The more inviting end of Dyckman Street ran in the opposite direction. The four blocks from Broadway to Nagle Avenue, where the IRT Subway emerged from Fort George Hill tunnel and began its elevated run to Van Cortlandt Park, were lined on both sides with stores: a Schulte United Cigar Store (that gave coupons); the Pork Store; a fish market; several open air fruit and vegetable stands; a variety of grocery stores, a Woolworth's Five and Ten; a Chinese restaurant; the Dew Drop Inn; Loew's Inwood movie house; a Thom McCann Shoe Store; Jack's Pants Shop; and a Knights of Columbus Hall. This strip was one of Inwood's two principal shopping and amusement centers (the other being 207th Street) and it always generated that special excitement associated with shopping.

15| Missy 3

MISSY AND WEST had been thinking about a home in the country. On the north shore of Long Island, in the summer community of Huntington Beach, they found a small frame house perched up on the hilltop of a long, wooded triangular lot. The house was elevated between two roads that dropped off into steep hills on either side and became one. The single road continued on down to the beach of Huntington Harbor.

The terrain of the small summer colony was rugged, and cottages were scattered here and there on the sandy hillsides ranging up from the water. Residents had built an open pavilion on the sand and pebble beach for bathers.

West arranged to have the house winterized so that it would be a year-round residence for Missy and West, a sanctuary from the hubbub and dirt of the City. Being some forty miles from Manhattan, it was not too long a trip either by rail or automobile. However, they decided to hold onto the 14th Street apartment. It would remain a small studio and business center for West. They settled into the Huntington Beach house with its new coal furnace and modernized plumbing in 1929.

Missy took up housekeeping in the new house while West, now spending less time at the Boathouse, commuted between 14th Street and Long Island. He had bought a Model A Ford coupe (with a rumble seat) to make the traveling back and forth easier. For a time, it looked as if Missy was going to learn how to drive too. This way the Ford could be garaged at the Huntington

Beach house and left for her convenience during the week. She could pick up or drive West to Huntington Station whenever he needed to be in the city or wanted to come out. Sadly, none of this worked out.

Missy either couldn't or wouldn't learn how to drive. West tried to teach her, my father tried to teach her. She'd get the car rolling for a while, then stall the engine shifting gears. She'd sit and laugh. The teachers gave up on her, and Missy never did learn how to drive.

Under the circumstances, West's trips to Huntington Beach grew less frequent. Missy complained. The family gave some thought to the matter and decided that if West had a studio room attached to the house, he could do most of his work right there at the house. So a vast, single room with casement windows on either side was added to the main house. The Swedish carpenters put up double glass doors and a balcony overlooking the great room with its raftered cathedral ceiling. They added a winding set of wooden stairs that turned down and opened out onto the great room's floor. They also constructed a huge, stone fireplace at the far end of the new room. With 18th century sword and fowling piece mounted over the mantle, the new studio room looked like the great hall of some English country manor house. All this was done, presumably, for West's benefit.

The addition was completed by the time Franklin Delano Roosevelt was elected for his first term as President. Like the national economy, the great hall turned unacceptably cold during the winter months. With all those windows, even a roaring fire in its fireplace wouldn't take the chill off it. As a result, the studio was usually closed off and, except for the summer months, West continued to drive to New York each week.

16| The Great Depression

A GOOD DEAL has been written about the Great Depression and of the Hard Times that went with it. My own introduction to the idea that something had gone wrong came by way of a black humor book that was circulating among the tenants at the Boathouse. As I remember, it was called "Fifty Ways to Commit Suicide." There were cartoon drawings of businessmen jumping out of office building windows, shooting themselves, hanging themselves or taking gas. Of course, the idea was to make light of misfortune. Some enterprising publisher had figured out a way to turn disaster to profit—possibly avoiding disaster for himself.

But whatever went bad during the Depression, the sense of it for us, the children of that generation in the midst of it, was not immediately clear in spite of the news stories. The collapse of the financial markets, the bank failures—they came suddenly. No one thought this crisis would last. We were just another family that had lost its money. We had been set back and had to make adjustments. If it was true that times were hard for us, they were hard for almost everybody else as well.

But a new way of thinking about things and a spirit of survival surfaced in the midst of it all. And with it, a broad sense of community. When the movie CAPTAINS COURAGEOUS played at the Loew's Inwood movie house, my father lent theater manager Goldfarb lanterns, oars, life rings and a boat compass for an advertising display. We got free passes to the theater for years to come, and the manager was always welcomed at the Boathouse.

It was the same with our family dentist, Shapiro and our insurance man, Rabinowitz—and Lou Holtzer, the peddler who taught me to play a C-scale on the cornet because my father allowed him to sell his wares at the Boathouse. It seemed as though people united to help one another in simple, unaffected and gratifying ways.

It might even be said that these same economic conditions that kept the nation and its people stagnant for so long also produced an orderly, simple and stable quality of life. Changes were wrought of necessity and were few. For years, subway fares, phone calls, hamburgers, hot dogs and soda pops were a nickel. And you could make a nickel by delivering a prescription for the Lippman, the pharmacist. As for us, the children of the Depression, we never thought of life as being any other way than it was as we grew up. We took our existence and simple pleasures to be normal because we had nothing to compare it with. And so, we didn't question it. We were no more deprived and had no less fun than children growing up in better times. In the end, I often think we were better off for it.

17| Locale 3

THE ATTRACTION OF Inwood Hill Park was of of a singular order. In the late 1920s and early 1930s, the thickly forested hill was populated only by institutional buildings and one or two private residences. Even then, it included one of the last patches of unspoiled land left on Manhattan Island. Ranging over the squatters' "Hooverville" shacks on the flats between the railroad tracks and the Hudson, the Hill ran some three quarters of a mile in a northerly direction from Dyckman Street's floor. As it reached Spuyten Duyvil Creek and the New York Central Railroad drawbridge, the hill looped around, its contours following the shoreline of the Creek. From the air, to a ballplayer, it might have looked like an old first baseman's mitt. The hill, as it turned into the crook of the thumb, overlooked a vast stretch of fields below which reached out into the Creek and Columbia University's Baker Field, and then the Broadway swing bridge. Further along, on the outside of the thumb, the hill offered a splendid view of the entire Vale of Inwood.

By the mid-thirties Inwood Hill Park had been taken over by the City. The institutional structures and the private dwellings were all torn down. Under a Depression public works program, the Park was restored to something like its original, natural woodland appearance. The City Parks Department put up two parkhouses and blacktopped and lighted the old footpaths. Planners added walls, steps, tunnels and rest area vistas for the convenience of strollers and sightseers who wanted to enjoy the

Park's 167 splendid acres of geological, historical and archeological wonders, and the spectacular views of the Hudson River and the Palisades.

The great attraction of Inwood Hill Park for us boys was its association with Indians, its splendid trees, its steep rock outcroppings, and its pungent black dirt in which grew scallions.

On our way to the summit of the park we often stopped to probe into the earth. Just under our feet we found specks of shell fragments, mute evidence that these hills were once entirely under water.

Arriving at the craggy outcroppings of Manhattan schist at the head of the Clove, we climbed to the great pot holes carved by the last glacier. We fitted into them with plenty of room to spare. Then we went on to climb to a place that was known by the tantalizing name of the Eagle's Nest. It was high above the Clove—a dangerous climb and a dangerous place to be. It was a mark of courage for a boy to climb to that point and crouch by the rock-slope for dear life, so of course we did it.

Indian Caves and Rock Shelters

Other times, we descended the steep path of the Clove that led to the Indian-life Reservation. Here we always stopped by the Indian caves and rock shelters. There was the usual challenge to see if we could fit through the narrow passages and to see how far back we could get into the caves (which always reeked of that pungent, outhouse smell of human feces). Tiring of this, we moved along to the Great Tulip Tree. Legend had it that Peter Minuit bought Manhattan Island from the Indians here for a handful of trinkets, some sixty guilders' worth.

The Great Tulip Tree was almost always the destination and the climax of any expedition into Inwood Hill Park. Some 250 years old when it died in 1938, the twin tines of its forked trunk rose to a height of 165 feet. It had been the oldest living thing on the Island of Manhattan, and it was the last link with the Reckgawawanc Indians who lived in this place, the Glen of Shorakapkok with its cold spring.

Once when I was very small, my mother took me on a walk through the Park to the Great Tree. Most residents and visitors of that time accepted the idea that there was an "Indian Village" at that location—or so they called it. Actually, there was a small stand by the Tree where three or four tattered, silent and dark people sold candy and small wooden objects to Sunday strollers. Someone pointed out the old woman and said that she was a princess, "a real Indian princess." Close by, was the cold spring that ran out from a stuccoed model of an Indian longhouse. The water bubbled cold and clear into a little pool made in the earth which was bordered by rocks. There was a crude dipper made from a tin cup sitting nearby for the stroller to fill with water and drink to refresh himself. Or, he might simply kneel down, lean over and put his face into the water.

I was awed by the idea that these were "real" Indians and was prepared to accept any story that anyone could tell of their ancestry. But my mother was quick to blot out any notion I had about these people being in any way noble or special. I asked if I could have a Hershey bar. My mother jerked me away and bent down to whisper: "They're dirty. Fooey! Dirty Indians . . . The candy has worms in it."

Princess Naomi and her grandchildren
in Inwood Hill Park, ca. 1930 (*Courtesy
of the New York Historical Society, New
York City*)

18| Bella

BELLA DREYFUS AT five was a chubby little girl with club legs, black hair and big round blue eyes. We had been put into the same 1st grade class at P.S. 52, Manhattan in ways that weren't planned much beyond class size in those beginning grades. Children were simply assigned to this class or that class and bonds were quickly established that often lasted throughout the primary and later, junior high school years. This is not to say that Bella was any more or less interesting to me than some other little girl or boy in our class. She was just one of twenty-five or so kids that I got quickly comfortable with, a familiar presence I could count on seeing almost every day, five days a week for 180 days of the school year. Bella, in that sense, was simply part of these new surroundings I was expected to fit into.

P. S. 52 Manhattan

From the outside, P.S. 52 with its massive red brick walls and stonework, its iron fences and gates looked in some respects like a medieval fortress—some have said prison. But the interior and particularly the classrooms were warm and protective. Perfect rows of iron-framed oak desks, each with its brass-lidded inkwell at the upper right corner, were bolted to well-scrubbed wooden floor boards. Yellow oak bookshelves were built into the back wall. Two sliding doors enclosed an oak wardrobe on the wall to our right. Inside, mounted on graduated oak strips, were cast iron hooks, each marked clearly with bold, black-stenciled numbers. Five great glass globes suspended from the high ceiling by chains lit the room while two tall metal-encased radiators on the window side heated the room. Four vast pole-manipulated windows on our left above the radiators took up almost all of that wall admitting light and air to the room and a view of the dingy tenement apartments across the street.

Every child who was assigned to that 1st Grade class had some identifying characteristic or some peculiarity that labeled him or her for years to come. It either had to do with what the kid looked like, what his name was or what he habitually did. Walter was the tallest kid in the class; David, the smallest. Vasilios had a name that was hard to pronounce and Patrick continued to talk when the teacher held her finger up to her lips for silence. Bella, aside from her big blue eyes, had a name that meant beautiful. But she was also frightened and unhappy about being in school and cried whenever the teacher asked her for an answer. This was what stuck in my mind about her—she was so terribly unsettled in her new surroundings, ones I thought altogether agreeable. And Bella's fear didn't diminish as those first weeks went by, and one day erupted into in one of those incidents that tend to fuse an early impression.

Some of us were chosen for parts in a Thanksgiving Day class play—little recitations to be memorized. On the Wednesday before the holiday we stood before the class to say our pieces on cue. The skinny little blond girl, Anna spoke her piece first.

Then it was Patrick the talker's turn, then mine. Next up was Bella.

There she stood, frozen in place looking vainly around for help. The teacher prompted, but still nothing came out of Bella's mouth. The room was quiet now and all eyes were on her. Then the trickle began. It ran down her leg and over her Mary Janes and onto the floor forming a little puddle. Boys in the back stood up to see—everyone saw it. Some children tittered; others sucked in their breath. But most just watched, waiting to see what would happen next.

Bella began to cry, quietly at first, then in one long wail. It was all over now. Poor Bella! But of course she was quickly forgiven and comforted by Mrs. McGinnis, one of those veteran teachers who ought to have been doing just what she was. Bella did recover and eventually found her way in school.

Now no one at that stage of life would condemn a classmate for an indiscretion, even of the magnitude of Bella's. We were all too involved with the newness of our own situations to cast stones at classmates. Still, early impressions backed by outward appearance, by some singular trait or as in the case of Bella, by some unfortunate incident left their mark. Identifying Patrick as a tongue-wagger or David as Squeaky was a simple, non-malicious expedient based on an observation that left an impression. So for better or worse, I got to think of Bella as Puddles. That outward show of her wretchedness and despair stayed with me for all the years we were together in P.S. 52.

Graduation from the Inwood Junior High School nine years later scattered the old familiar faces. Many of us chose high schools other than nearby George Washington to attend because of some special interest or aptitude. Just the same, we still encountered one another from time to time, one place or another in Inwood's precincts. And when this happened, that old bond of having watched one another grow up was always there and was always treated with a certain deference.

So it was, several years later, that I recognized Puddles one day on Broadway and Isham Street. I was quick to notice that at sixteen she had lost her baby fat—or at least had it redistributed to more attractive places. We recalled those first days in school and I felt comfortable enough to bring up her unhappy incident and the name I pinned on her as the result of it. She could laugh about it now and we were warmed at having seen one another again—grown up, as we liked to think.

19| Locale 4

AT THE SEAMAN Avenue end of the Spuyten Duyvil flats there was a vast field of fine, yellow dirt known to all of as Farmers Field. If you were a boy, this was the place you had to go to if you wanted to play serious sandlot baseball.

There were four vaguely traced baseball diamonds that fanned into one another. They seemed always to be occupied by some kids who had chosen up sides for an after-school or Saturday game.

On Sunday afternoon, on the principal field with its crude backstop cornering at Seaman Avenue and Isham Street, a lingering stroller in his church clothes might find a place on the stone cap of the wall above the field where he could sit and watch an organized game, complete with real bases and an umpire. Both teams were uniformed and came from somewhere else with their complement of equipment to play the local team.

Now and then, a familiar all-Black team came to play Sunday ball at Farmers Field. The team had a rangy, loose jointed pitcher everyone knew as Country Boy, and he was good. For baseball-minded youngsters, it was a special Sunday when Country Boy was on the mound. Every movement, gesture, sound and facial configuration was calculated. Country Boy had style. And to us, his performance was dazzling—hypnotic even. After the game we labored long and hard at mimicking his delivery. It became a game in itself. This was real baseball and we soaked it up knowing for a certainty that it had to make us good—maybe one day as good as Country Boy.

20| Vassy

MOST OF US who knew him well called him Vassy. At least in those first years of school. His real name was Vasilios. Vasilios Coulos. Vassy's parents were Greek and they ran a small restaurant at the corner of Broadway and 207th Street where he sometimes invited me to come after school on a winter's day to have a hot chocolate and a doughnut at the counter.

On my first day of school in P.S. 52, after an aborted few weeks in the first grade of a Jersey school at Lincoln Park, I was assigned to sit alongside Vassy. And from the 1st to the 6th grades we never sat very far apart from one another. I think it had something to do with the first letters of our last names being close together at the end of the alphabet. Or maybe it was because we were both about the same size. Whatever the reason, from the very beginning we took a shine to one another. I guess you could even say that a sort of friendly schoolboy rivalry developed between us, one that depended heavily on neither of us showing any of the characteristics of a "pyoik." *Pyoik* was our term for the later *bimmy*, and the modern equivalents of *nerd*, *wimp*, *wuss*, or *dweeb*.

Now, in those years penmanship was a daily part of our school instruction from grades one to four, and it was a skill that was taught with full attention to details and preparation. Every child at the beginning of the school year was given a simple wooden pen holder and two steel nibs—courtesy of the Board of Education of the City of New York. Each desk in the classroom had an inkwell in its upper right hand corner, and a dependable class-room monitor (a pyoik) at the beginning of each day passed from desk to desk with a large carboy and filled the little glass cup with pale blue ink. The round brass lids to the inkwells were to remain closed and to be opened only at filling times or during an official writing period. (Heh, heh.)

The first activity of the afternoon session was usually pen-manship. A sheet of white, blue-lined paper was passed back and laid on each desk. First, the teacher demonstrated how the pen was to be held: between thumb, index and second fingers with the remaining fingers curling inwards toward the thumb. Next, she directed our attention to the elbow and forearm. She demonstrated the gentle, sweeping arc made by using the elbow as a pivot. Now she had us lay the left arm on the desk above paper and the right arm with pen poised over it, being ever sure that the right elbow was also on the desk and never moved. We ran a few sweeps over the paper to get the feel of it while the teacher checked the way we were holding our pens and the way our arms worked. Finally she instructed us to open our inkwells and to dip the pen lightly into the ink, just to the point where the oval hole in the steel nib began. Only then were we ready to write.

The writing exercises began with long, sweeping arcs at the top of the page. Next came the circles: a line of forward circles, then a line of backward circles. The pen had always to be held at the proper angle and to glide lightly over the paper, otherwise its point would catch in the paper and flick ink spots on the page and very likely the hand of the writer. We did a line of U's and a line of M's; then a line of V's, staying always between the lines, yet still trying to touch them. Now, from the charts on the wall modeling the alphabet in Spencerian script, we wrote a line of connected a's, b's and so on. The teacher checked our work and ceremoniously stamped stars on the better papers.

A competition in penmanship began between Vassy and me. By the end of our first year in school we both had developed fine writing hands. And it was a question of pride to see who could write the neatest. But these tools we'd learned to use so well to write with soon found other uses. The delicate instrument that produced such fine letters on paper, if launched properly, would stick nicely in the wooden floor—like a dart of sorts. The paper too had secondary uses. If folded in a certain way it became a snapper. And if torn into strips and folded tightly and then dipped into ink, it became a missile that could be launched with a rubber band.

Punchball was by far the game of preference in P.S. 52's great schoolyard, and Vassy had to be one of its outstanding players. Punchball was a game modeled after baseball, but played with a rubber ball and without a pitcher. As many as twenty kids chose up sides during recesses, at gym periods and during lunch hours. The batter stepped up to home plate, chalked on the concrete square, bent low, dropped the ball, and with the inside of his fist hit it on the rise trying to keep it away from fielders. The hitter was successful if he could speed the ball on a low roll between two infielders and on into the outfield. No one I knew could do this better than Vassy. First he'd find the hole he was looking for. Then in one motion he'd crouch low, hold the ball out with his left hand and let it bounce no higher than an inch or two from the ground. Then he'd slam it with his right hand sending it on a perfect roll between the infielders for an easy double or triple if the outfielder happened to bobble it. And if Vassy excelled as a hitter, he ran and moved in the outfield just as well, throwing the ball back with unfailing accuracy and speed.

Actually, I think both of us developed good throwing arms in those first years of school when the original Ward 52 school building at Broadway and Academy Street was abandoned for remodeling. There was a vacant lot behind it then, with piles of rubble. I can remember standing there one afternoon after school for two hours challenging Vassy at lofting rocks at the remaining panes of glass up on the third floor. To a boy that age there is probably nothing more gratifying than to throw a rock and watch it rise and hear it smash a piece of glass some thirty yards away.

In the early grades the single advantage one kid held over another was swiftness of motion and speed afoot. The fast kid always held the upper hand over the stronger kid because he could duck out of the way and run from possible harm. Vassy was fast like that, and fast in other ways. On a school line he could tear the button fly in your knickers wide open before you could move. Or he could grab your hat and duck under you when you reached for him. Other times he'd say, "See where the horse bit me?" He'd show you his shoulder with one hand and squeeze you in the crotch with the other. Another gag: a quick feint and he had you. "You flinched! Two for flinching"—two fingers slapped across the inside of your wrist as hard as he could exact the penalty.

It was a dull day, one of those autumn days when I didn't want to go straight home from school. I stayed on in the schoolyard, even though I'd been told I had to come "straight home" and change my clothes. Four or five of us kids began a game of tag. Vassy was one of them. I was "it" and was chasing him. He ducked and dodged out of my reach time after time frustrating me. I could never seem to catch him. At last I caught the end of his open coat. He pulled away and I slipped and went face down onto the concrete. I felt him helping me up. I said thanks and noticed that the inside of my mouth felt different. Vassy looked long at me with eyes and mouth wide open. "Your front teeth . . . They're broke," he said finally. Something gave way inside me and I began to cry—not from any pain I felt, but from what I knew my mother would say.

Now Vassy had always been a loyal school friend as I saw it. So I decided I owed it to him not to involve him in my unfortunate accident. My mother would surely pin a good part of the blame on him: "One of those damn kids you hang around with." (It always bothered me when she said that.) So on the long walk home I devised an elaborate tale of how I jumped for a pipe bar over a fence gate that was open at the time and missed, cracking my teeth against the bar. This was good all right, but I was still terrified thinking about how my mother would react when she finally noticed my saw teeth.

I came down the ramp and into the Boathouse and slipped past by my father who was at work on an outboard motor in his shop. I went on through the main house and climbed the narrow, steep wooden steps to our little apartment and opened the door quietly. My mother was back in the kitchen getting supper ready. As quiet as I was, she still heard me come in. "Where've you been?" she asked.

"You won't get mad if I show you something?" I said.

I knew that my appeal would do no good—of course she knew immediately that something was terribly wrong. She stopped what she was doing and said, "What? Show me what?" I watched her expression change, her eyes narrowing. I knew then I was in for it. I opened my mouth and showed her the gaping hole between my two front teeth. Her eyes opened wide. "Oh, my God!" she groaned, "You . . . What did you do?" She grabbed at the first kitchen utensil she could find and flung it at me. I covered my head, needlessly as it turned out because the potato masher went wild slamming into the wall. My mother broke into sobs.

Well, anyway, my fabrication as to how this terrible thing happened held up. Vassy was in the clear. My account really wasn't that far from the truth, I told myself. And, I wouldn't have to hear about how I was being led astray by "muckers."

21| Locale 5

THE WAY I saw it, Inwood Hill Park stood watch over the vale of Inwood as a sort of sentinel. A handful of blocks spread out below the Hill to the east. The alleyways of Academy Street, West 204th, West 207th and Isham Streets were crossed by Seaman Avenue, Cooper Street, Broadway, Vermilyea, Sherman, Post and Nagle Avenues to make rectangles. Tenth Avenue, from the Sherman's Bay inlet, to where it joined Broadway at West 218th Street belonged to the City's 1811 block pattern for the Borough of Manhattan. It ran straight and at about a thirty degree angle from Inwood's own grid. The little streets ranging off it to the north, West 201st Street to West 220th Street, joined Tenth Avenue and broken Ninth Avenue at right angles in accord with the City Plan. They made kind of an eastern frame to Greater Inwood, these flatlands along the Harlem. The little streets were mostly broken into by the New York City Transit's car barns and sidings. At the southern end of the cut of Sherman's Bay, stood the four-stack Edison Power plant. Alternately, filling in the spaces, there were scattered several three story tenements.

The hills of Isham Park and the heights of Park Terrace were somehow exotic places for our little gang. These were Catholic strongholds presided over by red-faced priests and whispering nuns who served the churches and schools of Good Shepherd and the Sacred Heart of Mary. We were sure that the priests and nuns warned their charges to keep away from us. We imagined that there were sacred rites and mysteries going on in these carefully monitored places, things we could never understand or become any part of. Somehow we knew we didn't belong in these reserved spaces. We were respectful, a little awed and a little afraid. And so we kept our distance.

22| Boathouse Row

WHERE THE VAST, cobblestoned expanse of Dyckman Street fanned out at the Hudson River's edge there was an el-shaped pier that extended out over the water. It was the old Tubby Hook dock. By the 1930s it was no longer in use as a terminal and was left to the public as a fishing pier and a place to walk to and cool off on a hot summer evening. Just above the dock there was a sewage disposal plant that, depending upon the direction of the wind, thickened the air with the smell of solid wastes. Running south of Dyckman Street from the ferry slip, along the edge of the river and below the New York Central's tracks there was a narrow, rutted roadway that had no name. Along it there was a string of boathouses, one after the next along the road until the road became a footpath through tall reeds and ended finally in jagged rockfill along the water's edge at Fort Washington Point.

I was alway embarrassed when I had to clarify my address at school. In the first place, I was never quite sure what it was— officially, that is. My teachers were always at a loss when they saw no street name and number in the address I gave them. "Foot of Dyckman Street and Hudson River" didn't seem to cover it somehow, leaving me to explain the boathouse business. The teachers were always interested in this, but invariably stumbled over the boathouse part. In their minds, I lived in a "houseboat" and it could never be any other way.

Each of the wooden houses and sheds along Boathouse Row could be quickly identified by color. As you left the ferry slip and made your way along the black, oiled, ash-fill of the narrow roadway, you came immediately to the bright green of O'Connor's Boathouse. Next, was West's (later T. Roberts), the yellow boathouse where we lived. Then came the gray, Inwood Boat & Canoe Club, the only house without storage sheds. The red house, the Weona Yacht Club, belonged to Charlie De George and his family. It was the only boathouse to have a bar and the drunks to go with it. Last in the line was the orange house occupied by old man Cox. The largest of all the houses along Boathouse Row, it burned to the ground in a spectacular fire in 1935 and was never rebuilt.

Each house along Boathouse Row had staked floats accessible by wooden gangways. These rose and fell with the tides and had to be swung up on the decking in October or November for the winter months, and to be put out once again the following spring. In our boathouse, the floats, their stakes removed, were pulled around to the end of the house into the cut and anchored there. At low tides during the boating season, the floats barely raised above the thick, black muck of the river bed below them making the gangway angle steep and dangerous. In fact, splinters—not to mention carelessly discarded cigarette butts were always a hazard with wooden decking all around the houses and sheds.

The boathouses along Boathouse Row served mainly as storage areas for canoe and small boat owners. There were moorings set out too for owners of larger cabin craft. Dock space was limited at the smaller boathouses. Usually a tenant was provided with either a rack for his canoe or deckspace for his outboard boat. He had a locker assigned to him and paid a monthly rent, depending upon the kind of accommodation he needed for his boat. Some owners preferred their boats to be stored in the sheds on dollies which meant a higher rent.

It ought to be said somewhere in here that the Hudson River was unspeakably dirty at this time. In spite of sewage treatment plants, raw sewage drifted back and forth with every change of the tide. Boathouses (including ours) freely flushed their waste and dropped their garbage directly into the river. Driftwood, condoms called "Hudson River white eels," or more crudely, "scum bags," oil caked feces all collected into a line commonly referred to as "the shit line." Swimmers (and there were those) were advised to swim at high tides and to master the Hudson River Crawl, a stroke where the chin was always well out of the water and where the arms reached out in front of the swimmer sweeping the sludge away before him.

23| The Boathouse Gang

THE YOUNG MEN who stored their boats and canoes at the Boathouse, once they were settled in, usually stayed for a long time and became part of the Boathouse Gang. On summer nights when the air in the streets was still, they liked to come by with their wives and girlfriends to sit quietly along the dock, smoking and talking, cooling off over the water. Sometimes they came to gather around the radio to listen to the latest Joe Louis heavyweight fight being fought only a few miles away at the Polo Grounds or Yankee Stadium. And they were there too, these faithful tenants, as they promised they would be on the days my father set aside to put out or take in the floats. They even found their way to the Boathouse through the ice and the snow on the coldest days of winter when the river was frozen solid except for the shipping and ferry lanes. On those days the more spirited ones climbed out onto the ice jams, seeing how close they could get to the moving ice. The others, less adventurous, used the Boathouse as a clubhouse playing ping pong or working on the ever expanding HO gauge model railroad by the wood burning stove.

In the great days of the cedar canoe and double spoon-bladed paddles, the ultimate adventure was to get four or five canoes lined up in tandem and to hitch a ride up the Hudson tied to the end of a barge. For some reason that was never clear to me, the preferred camping spot for this canoe trip was always a place called Eddyville. (I have never been able to find it on a map.) After leaving off the barge, Eddyville meant a fair amount of paddling into the Rondout Creek south of Kingston. There must have been a lively camp ground at some point around there because the gang always came back Sunday night with a host of stories to tell of their experiences. These tales would be milked of their essence again and again in the intervening weeks until the next trip.

Dangerous sport with a canoe was to ride the wave in the wake of the ferry. Only skilled canoeists who had learned how to maneuver quickly with their doubles paddles attempted to do this. The idea was to get directly behind the ferry as close as possible and to hold the canoe steady. The trick was not to lose the wave, to stay on it. If you were successful you'd ride all the way across the river to Jersey with the ferry. The dangerous part was that you could be drawn into the paddle wheels when the ferry slowed and the paddles reversed. One summer two boys drowned, not knowing enough to break off the roll at the right time. Not many tried this stunt after that.

The Halloween Party

The grand event of the year at the Boathouse was the annual Halloween party. All tenants and Boathouse regulars were invited. It was a costume party with a prize for the most original costume. For the occasion the regular entrance to the Boathouse was converted to a gauntlet, and every new entrant had to run it. It was a darkened, narrow tunnel with jack-o-lanterns, skeletons, scare noises and electric shocks placed at strategic points. To the welcome cheers of the already initiated, the new arrivals emerged into the lights of the main house now decorated with orange and black streamers, apples on strings, apples floating in tubs of water and Halloween masques pinned everywhere on the walls. The gang danced to records I played for them on an amplified pick-up. And for this one occasion, there was liquor allowed, even encouraged, at the Boathouse.

24| O'Connell

O'CONNELL WAS the name everyone knew him by. He was a happy drunk with bad teeth who snorted when he laughed, probably trying to choke off the alcohol fumes that always hung about him. But he was an amiable sort and everyone at the Boathouse knew him and liked him. He didn't store a boat with us or at any of the other houses on Boathouse Row. Like the tide, O'Connell just drifted in and out regularly.

It was generally believed that O'Connell was a newspaper man, though what kind of work he did for what newspaper was never known. Whenever he showed up at the Boathouse he always wore a dark suit with a white shirt and tie, and he was never without his grey fedora hat giving the impression that he had just come from work—after a visit to one or more of Inwood's numerous bar & grills.

One sunny afternoon early in September O'Connell had absorbed more than his usual quantity of whiskey before he weaved his way into the Boathouse. One of the boys returning from a canoe trip had folded out his army cot on the large float to air out the canvas. O'Connell, having grinned through the routine pleasantries, found the cot and asked its owner if it would be okay for him to stretch out on it in the sun for a few minutes. There was no objection. So O'Connell settled back on the canvas tipping his fedora forward over his eyes, and, lulled by the lapping of the waves under the float, promptly wafted into a profound sleep.

The tide had turned and the waters of the Hudson began to

move down river. O'Connell slept on undisturbed by the remarks directed at him by the boys landing their boats as they passed by his cot. The driftwood in the river moved faster now, and a tenant named Henry, who had just lifted his cedar canoe onto the float, noticed a massive flat surface as it turned past the ferry slip. Caught in the eddy currents, it moved in toward the boathouses. Henry called to his friend Sponse up on the dock to come look. It was a section of a dock, an old ferry landing they thought. They ran for the boat hook to pull it in for a closer look. A few others gathered around. They strained to hold it to the float by its one remaining cleat. In the struggle, someone suddenly became aware of O'Connell, still sound asleep. The idea flashed through minds simultaneously. Gently, two boys lifted the cot with O'Connell on it while the others who came to watch held the makeshift raft to the float. They set the cot well to the center of the raft and pushed it back out into the river where the current gathered it up once again in its flow southward.

Back up on the decking, they stood in a group passing the binoculars from one to the other, watching for a sign of life from O'Connell. There was none. The raft drifted passed Cox's, the last boathouse in the row, and was moving rapidly toward the George Washington Bridge. The laughter suddenly stopped. Sponse readied his outboard for the pick-up, but he was too late. A passing tug had spotted the raft, now well out in the river and moving fast, and angled toward it.

A crewman in the bow of the tug hailed the raft, but its passenger was still sound asleep. Coming alongside, the captain issued orders to have the man pulled aboard. It was a fumbling maneuver, carried out without care. Inevitably, the raft tipped and the legs of the cot slid. Into the waters of the Hudson went O'Connell. Lines and boathooks went quickly over the side. The tug crew finally got the choking O'Connell up over the gunwales, suit and fedora soaking wet.

The captain of the tug hailed a passing outboard boater who carried the sputtering O'Connell to solid ground at Fort

Washington Point under the Bridge. He trudged his way back over the rocks, along the path into the roadway of Boathouse Row and into the Boathouse.

"Who did this to me?" O'Connell tried to sound angry, holding his arms out, looking down at his sagging clothes and occasionally snorting his special laugh. He wanted everyone who stood around him laughing to know that he wasn't really angry and could take a joke as well as the next guy.

25| Locale 6

SOMETHING OF AN historic record of Inwood and Marble Hill is preserved in the names of its streets. Dyckman Street and Nagle (sic) Avenue were named for Jan Dyckman and his partner Jan Nagel who in 1677 acquired the boweries, or farmlands, of Tobias Teunissen, a native of Leyden and the first white man to settle in this locality. Teunissen's lands were abandoned in 1655 when he and all but one of his family were slaughtered by Weckquaesgeek (Wicker's Creek ?) Indians because he had served as a guide for Governor Keift's military expedition against the Indians in 1642. He is memorialized by Teunissen Place in Marble Hill at the approximate site where he lived.

Seaman Avenue, opened in 1908 and extended in 1912, was named for the family of Henry B. Seaman. The Seaman Family Estate consisted of some twenty-five acres from Park Terrace Hill to Spuyten Duyvil Creek.

Academy Street was named for the first school in Inwood. The school was built in 1857 and dedicated in 1858. As Ward School 52, it was called MacKean's Folly for the city school commissioner responsible for its construction because its three stories were so sparsely populated when the school first opened its doors. Later, under the five-borough, Greater New York reorganization it became Public School 52, Manhattan. The old building, having been remodeled several times still stands at its original location at the corner of Broadway and Academy Street.

Payson Avenue, originally Prescott Avenue, was named for

George Shipman Payson, pastor of the Mount Washington Church from 1874 to 1920. The avenue which borders on Inwood Hill Park from Dyckman Street to where it feeds into Seaman Avenue cuts through the site of a former British military encampment, the 17th Foot Regiment of 1778. Many relics were found when the street was laid as a continuation of former F Street.

Riverside Drive, originally called Lafayette Boulevard, was named for the young French marquis who lent aid to the colonials during the American Revolution.

Vermilyea Avenue was named for Isaac Vermilyea or Vermeille, a settler of Italian descent who arrived in New Harlem in 1662. He became a constable and a magistrate, and by 1712 owned a sizeable tract of land.in Inwood Hill Park.

The Sherman Family lived on the south side of a small bay later named for them. They also gave their name to Inwood's longest avenue.

During the 19th century a few of Inwood's streets were named for popular American writers. West 204th Street was originally Hawthorne Street and West 207th, Emerson Street. The only street that didn't undergo a name-to-number change was Cooper Street, named for James Fenimore Cooper.

No discussion of the streets and avenues of Inwood would be complete without some mention of Broadway. Following the old Weckquaesgeek Path, the artery ran all the way from one end of the thirteen-mile length of Manhattan Island to the other and was commonly known as the Bloomindale Road. When it reached the prominent triangle where it joined the Dyckman Street and Riverside Drive of today, by one of those small brooks that then ran across the valley floor from Sherman's Bay, it turned to the east and over to the Muscoota, or Harlem flats. From here it followed the Harlem River shoreline to the banks of the meandering Spuyten Duyvil Creek where, at low tide at one point, a traveler could make a crossing on foot. The Indians had called the ford the Wading Place. It was located near the present intersection of Broadway and 230th Street.

The crossing soon became important to travel between Manhattan and the mainland, both to points to the north and to the east of it. In 1667, near this strategic location, Governor Nicolls, by the approval of the Township of New Harlem, directed that a toll ferry to the mainland be established and maintained. Factious New Yorkers paid scant attention, continuing to cross at the shallows as they had always done. Town officials insolently built fences. They were just as soon torn down by enraged farmers who had cattle to move.

Then in 1669, Johannes Verveelen, a New Harlem patentee who had built his house on a town lot on the north side of the Creek, then called Paparinemin Island, petitioned for and was appointed Ferryman. Wisely, he converted his house into a tavern. And he, himself, served for many years as Ferryman and tavern keeper at this important junction. Verveelen was relieved of his post in 1692 and died in 1702. Only little Verveelen Place in the Kingsbridge section of the Bronx is left to mark the station he kept for twenty-three years.

In the first years of the 18th century, a new patent was granted to Frederick Philipse by King William the Third. The old ferry was abandoned and Philipse, within a year's time, built a toll bridge in place of the ferry. In honor of his patron, he named it the King's Bridge.

In 1713, Philipse replaced the original toll bridge with a larger, sturdier drawbridge. Controlled by the British during the Revolution, this was the bridge that George Washington crossed on his way south to take New York back from the British on November 27, 1783—Evacuation Day.

Patriots lined the route and cheered as Washington and his war-weary troops from the Newburgh cantonment made their way along the Kings Bridge road into Inwood and up to the Heights later named for him.

During the 19th century the Bloomindale Road was extended more directly northwards through Inwood. By 1850, it sloped downwards from Washington Heights, then bowed its way around to the Dyckman-Riverside Drive intersection. From here it now followed in a more or less straight line into Marble Hill. The Kings Bridge Road, as it became known in Inwood, replaced the old Indian path over to the Harlem flats.

By 1895 with the new Ship Canal and later landfill of the original creek bed, the old Marble Hill bridge site disappeared entirely. Some ten years later engineers built a new swing bridge over the Canal for the IRT Elevated with a lower roadbed for the streetcar line and wide enough on either side for cars and trucks. Old Kings Bridge Road was virtually abandoned at the Canal cut and became a minor road. It was called alternately Marble Hill Avenue, then Kingsbridge Avenue, and it ended at West 238th Street where it fed into today's Broadway. Finally, the great artery was called Broadway over its entire length from the Battery of lower Manhattan to Inwood, then on to Yonkers and beyond where it became the Albany Post Road, later to be identified on road maps simply as U.S. Route 9.

26| Up the Street

"UP THE STREET" was the operative phrase, the catch-all response to the question "Where are you going?" There was no need to specify further. The response could have no other meaning than up Dyckman Street and to some yet undetermined location in Inwood depending upon whom I might meet and where we decided to go. In effect, it meant I was leaving Boathouse Row to seek out my friends, kids my own age, for there were none here.

If the phrase was challenged at all, the qualifier was either "Not until you . . ." or, "Be back here by . . ." All this was, of course, pro forma and anticipated. It was part of the ritual of going "up the street" and had no further significance other than a possible brief delay while someundone task was attended to. But the walk itself, which I always had to take to school, and which I might have taken at least one more time each day, was never without some promise. There were always those familiar things I could expect to see and still other things that were entirely new and therefore interesting.

The rutted road of Boathouse Row by this time had a railroad tie bulkhead some five feet high running the length of the road opposite the boathouses. The bulkhead served to hold the new elevation of the New York Central's rumbling freight line in place. It was both a change and a challenge to walk along on those uneven top ties once in a while. Or sometimes De George's mutt, Yaller Dog, would come barking after me. I didn't mind this at all because it gave me the excuse to heave a rock or snowball in his direction and hear him yelp when it hit which, unfortunately, was not often enough.

Tromping over the cracks in the heavy boards of the ferry slip, I turned past the Greek's hot dog stand and into Dyckman Street. I went under the girdered railroad bridge and later-added Henry Hudson Parkway overpass. The sidewalk underneath these structures was always spattered with pigeon dung and on zero-degree days, I could count on seeing a dead pigeon frozen solid on the sidewalk. I glanced up to look at the familiar grafitti on the concrete wall. I thought to myself it must have taken the writer some time to paint that legend on that rough surface. It was neatly done too, though I had no idea at the time what it meant:

Oh, John, let's not park here.
Oh, John, let's not park.
Oh, John, let's not.
Oh, John, let's.
Oh, John.
Oh . . . Utter Silence

I passed by the New York Central red brick power sub-station with its ominous, humming transformers and warning signs. No one ever seemed to be there. I often wondered what actually went on inside its dark and secret recesses. The next landmark was across Staff Street, the corner garage and warehouse with the green Quaker Oil sign standing in front of it suspended in its metal frame. I never passed this sign without whanging it with the end of my fist or with some stick I had chanced to pick up. To me the sound it made came close enough to the sound I figured a Chinese gong would make, and that satisfied me. At Henshaw Street it was time to cross the street to the park side.

Just ahead of me, where the park leveled out at Payson Avenue, was a construction site. WPA workers were cranking portable generators into life and setting up board walkways for their wheel barrows. The City of New York had taken over Inwood

Hill Park, and the old private residences, the Jewish Memorial Hospital and the other institutional buildings had already been torn down. Bolton Road was being lined on its lower side with a rugged stone wall. Below it, a park house of red brick with limestone corners and a blue slate roof was being put up along Dyckman Street. A small sandlot facing the park house had already been turned into a fenced-in playground with see-saws and swings. The old trees were left and new trees were being planted for additional shade along Dyckman Street and Payson Avenue. Both outside and inside the playground, concrete bench frames were being anchored at strategic intervals for mothers and strollers alike. All in all, the site added up to a pleassant prospect for a kid to do some poking around in.

I landed on the familiar wide apron of Dyckman Street and looked up Payson Avenue. Would any of the kids from the gang be out already and around the block? I spotted Izzie Katzenberg making his way into the courtyard of The Charles apartments with a suit draped over his back. He was the oldest of the Katzenbergs, the tailor's son who would be delivering a suit for his father. I continued up Dyckman. I saw Alex, the youngest of the Katzenbergs, inside the shop talking to his red-haired mother as I passed. He was my age and in my class at school, but here on the block we had little to do with one another. I waved hello.

I went past the rest of the storefronts along Dyckman Street and headed up Seaman Avenue. I turned down the familiar steep ramp by the ash cans and entered the cellar of 2-12 Seaman where I once lived. Intuitively I knew that Ole would be home. Most likely we'd find the others in the park later.

27| Locale 7

THE TENTH AVENUE elevated structure of the IRT Subway intersected Broadway at 218th Street and continued northward until it crossed the Creek's canal-cut into Marble Hill by the old Broadway drawbridge. Marble Hill and the opposite shores of Spuyten Duyvil were still familiar territory to us. There we found twisting roads and hills we could explore. We could go down to the old Spuyten Duyvil railroad station, and then up to the heights above the Creek that looked out across the Hudson to the majestic Palisades. We knew the place, wrongly, as Riverdale. Actually, it would be many years before we would roam the Hudson heights as far north as Riverdale.

The definitive exit to the other nation called the Bronx was the 207th Street University Heights swing bridge with its trolley tracks. The zig-zag hill on the opposite side of the Harlem River as it reached University Heights became, properly, Fordham Road. New York University's Bronx Campus's Hall of Fame which overlooked the Harlem and our Inwood community was acceptable roaming terrain for us. But if we continued much beyond here, we knew we would be ranging into foreign lands.

We always thought of the Bronx as a great, nondescript residential hodge-podge—a place where people hid in their apartments while they weren't at work or shopping. Bronx kids never seemed to use their streets to play in, as we had done with Payson Avenue. Bronx streets were merely conduits serving as passageways from one place to the next.

At seven or eight years of age, Fordham Road and the Bronx itself was at best only good for a movie house showing a Marx Brothers movie or the Bronx Zoo. As a result, we spent precious little of our time over there.

28| Ole 2

AS WE BEGAN school at P.S. 52 Manhattan, we boys felt more emancipated and began to wander more. I was settled in at the Boathouse now and, as explained, had always to walk "up the street" to be with any of my friends. Soon the adventures I shared with Ole Swensen spread out well beyond the apartment building at 2-12 Seaman Avenue.

In the beginning, our roving took in only the familiar Seaman-Beak-Payson-Dyckman block and its alleyways between the apartment buildings. Later, we explored the nearer hillsides of Inwood Hill Park. We played along Bolton Road, where Ole had broken his limbs at an earlier time, and now went up into the park as far as the ruins of the recently razed Jewish Memorial Hospital. It was a challenge to climb over the rubble in the cluttered below-ground passageways that had yet to be filled in. On longer expeditions we followed Seaman Avenue over most of its length to Farmers Field to watch a baseball or a football game. And as we got older, inevitably we went farther in what I suppose you could call impromptu drifting.

It was a blustery Saturday afternoon in April when Ole and I decided to take a leisurely walk across the 207th Street bridge into the foreign lands of the Bronx. Our goal was uncertain at first. We stood on the Bronx shore opposite the Edison power plant and found a couple of sticks to smack rocks into the Harlem River. Without thinking much about it we drifted over to Sedgwick Avenue and before long found ourselves gazing into the shiny faces of the bronze busts at New York University's Hall of Fame. We could read them, but the names meant nothing to us. We amused ourselves for a time trying to prounounce them and ended up by inventing rhyming parodies as children so often do. It was still early and the sun was still well up in the sky. We decided to go on with our walk. Wasn't the Bronx Zoo around here somewhere?

We went back to Fordham Road and followed the trolley tracks that climbed to University Heights. Passing Saint Nicholas of Tolentine R.C. church, we went under the el at Jerome Avenue. We crossed the Grand Concourse then descended the store-lined blocks of Forham Road to the cluttered square at Webster Avenue where Rogers Department Store cornered. The trolleys crossed by one another dinging their bells while cars and trucks waited for openings to get by them. Now, we weren't at all sure where the zoo was, but it couldn't be very far away. Ole and I walked on with renewed purpose.

The two of us went under the el at Third Avenue and passed Roosevelt High School. Just across from it was the walled-in campus of Fordham University. Crossing Southern Boulevard, there before us at last was the gilded gate entrance to the Bronx Zoo.

It was near closing time, but Ole and I were able to run through the Lion House and stop by the cage with the great apes to stare at a gorilla who looked bored. Without warning our legs beginning to stiffen and lose control. We were suddenly reminded that it was a long way back—and it was getting dark.

We'd never make it home in time for supper. Our parents would be worried and there'd be problems, we knew. Exhausted and frightened and without any money, neither of us could figure out what to do. Dejected, we sat down on a bench outside the park. At least we would rest our tired legs.

A cop leaving the zoo noticed us. We must have looked lost. "What're youse kids hangin' around heah fa? Hah? You waitin' fa somebody?" We explained our situation, "C'mon," said the cop. He lead us to the trolley stop and an X-car. "Git on," he said, then exchanged a few words with the motorman. Turning back to us: "Don't never do nothin' like this again," he pointed a finger at us, "y'unnerstan'? . . . An when yez git awp da car, yez go right home . . . Ya got that?" We got it.

Ole and I were late for our supper just the same. But we had figured out on the trolley ride back to Inwood that it was probably a good idea not to elaborate on our adventure, great though it was. It would only cause our parents a lot of needless worry. (If they only knew the trouble we went to to keep them from doing that.)

29| Missy 4

MISSY'S STATUS IN the family did not diminish, even though the immediate family was reunited in the Boathouse. It was a role that was altered, to be sure, from her familiar and regular presence of years past. But while Missy wasn't there at the Boathouse as much anymore, our tenants behaved as if she were. They asked after her, signaling that she was missed. When she did show up for a visit, it was as if she'd never left. She was still recognized as the director and senior partner whether she was there or not. And if anything, my fascination with and attraction for Missy grew stronger.

To the wider family, the Huntington Beach house came to be a sort of holiday house. Summer days to be sure. But it was also here that the family gathered to celebrate the Thanksgiving or Christmas holiday. And it was also here where my mother knew she could leave me for the rest of the week without worrying that I would get homesick. As in most such cases it was a good arrangement for all parties concerned. My mother was freed from the daily grind of managing a household with me as the worry spot. And Missy was glad to have me around.

My earliest recollections of those holiday visits are inevitably tied to the long drive from the Boathouse to Huntington Beach in the great square family Buick. We left off Broadway and turned down 207th Street trying to stay off the slippery surfaces of the trolley tracks that threw the car from side to side as we crossed the narrow bridge over the Harlem River into the Bronx. Then we climbed to University Heights where we continued on Fordham Road past the shopping center. We turned south at White Plains Road and made our way to the line of cars waiting at the Clason Point ferry slips.

The ferry ride across the East River to Long Island was a long one, though not a dull one. Vagabond musicians serenaded us playing the popular hits of the day. Swarthy accordian, mandolin and guitar players drifted between the cars playing.the popular song hits of the day: "Louise" or "Singing in the Rain" or "You're Driving Me Crazy." Before we docked, the mustacheod men jingled tin cups by the car windows. They knew who would pay and waited patiently for those motorists to fish out and plunk their coins into the cups. There were vendors on the ferry too. "Es-kee-mo pies," they cried, with their dry ice containers strapped over their shoulders. "Es-kee-mo pies . . . Get your Es-kee-mo pies he-uh!" I took in the entire show from my car window without being bored in the slightest.

The second stage of the journey began at the ferry landing in College Point. The Causeway took us to an intersection with Northern Boulevard in Flushing which we followed eastward until it became 25A. This unglamourous alphanumeric designation imbedded itself in my mind as the way to Huntington Beach. After several trips I memorized in order the more exotic names of the landmarks we passed: Little Neck, Manhasset, Roslyn, Oyster Bay, Cold Spring Harbor and its "Fitch" hatchery.

After an eternity of rutching on someone's lap, I settled to stillness as we rolled past the Sears Roebuck store and into Huntington's Main Street. This meant that we were almost there. Out in the country once again, I knew that we had to take the left fork at the Greenlawn Road intersection, go around the Crescent Club golf course and make that final right turn at the head of the hill. It would be the first house on the left. There was a drop, then a turn into the short driveway in front of the double-doored garage.

Before the car could come to a complete stop Missy was out of the house wrapped in her holey, button-front gray wool sweater,

arms out, clapping, laughing, coughing—her hoarse voiced bellowing, "Hello, hello . . . You're here! Hooray, hooray!" Now in
the house, with voices trapped in the small rooms, and with everyone speaking his piece at once, greetings were exchanged. It was
all a part of the ceremony, the noise of the seasonal warming up.

If it wasn't too cold, we might celebrated the holiday with the
traditional turkey dinner served on the balcony overlooking the
great studio room. West and my father coaxed up a blazing fire in
the great stone fireplace at the far end of the room to take the
chill off the air. Soon there was the convivial smell of burning
wood. Grandpa Freudiger and Cousin Walter, both Switzers with
an eye for detail, clucked admiration in French over West's pen
and ink drawings that hung on the stuccoed walls. Missy and my
mother busied themselves with the dinner preparations and place
settings on the long table that had been leafed-out to accommodate
the expanded family.

At last it was time for Missy's parade through the house while
she sang out loud with her raspy voice: "Ready, ready . . .
Everybody to the table, (insistent) Come on now." We took our
assigned places and my father ran a corkscrew into Grandpa
Freudiger's bottle of Neuchâtel. Glasses went up and we toasted
another holiday together and sat for the business of eating.

Now began the ritual of the carving of the turkey. The job
went naturally to Grandpa Freudiger as the oldest man in the
gathering. Or maybe it was just because he was good at carving.
He sliced thin with the knack of one who had been around restaurants for most of his life, which indeed he was—he had been
maître d' in some of London's and New York's finest restaurants.

Now came the passing of the platters with Missy in total command. She never missed an opportunity to badger: "Don't be
stingy now . . . Here, give me that . . . Don't you want any dressing?" She waited for the corrections to be made and until all the
plates were filled as she determined they ought to be. Only then
did the family dare to begin eating.

The food went down fast. Missy signaled to this one or that

one to take more. The eating went on until the plates were empty and the seats were pushed back from the table. There were the usual groans and grunts of satiation. Everybody was contentedly stuffed. It's curious though, as I think back on it now, I can't remember ever having seen Missy eat a single mouthful. Yet there was her plate, as empty as the rest.

While I resigned myself to the fact that I was the only child in this family of adults, I quickly grew bored and restless with grown-up talk. I asked to be excused from the table while the others, full of food, remained seated to smoke and reflect on the state of world affairs. Content to have the whole great studio room to myself for my solitary entertainment, I pulled out West's illustrated reference books and flipped pages until I got tired of this. Then I rearranged sofa cushions on a pile in the middle of the floor and dived into them, lifting myself as high as I could. When I wearied of that, I made a house of the cushions, crawled in and fell asleep.

Other times, West might take a hand at entertaining me. He lifted the old Civil War sword down from over the fireplace and showed me how it slipped in and out of its rusty scabbord warning me to be careful of the blade. There wasn't much danger I'd get hurt though. The sword was too dull and too heavy. Yet it was fun just to drag it along behind me pretending to be some important military personage.

If the weather was good and not too cold, the visiting family led by West walked down the steep hill to the beach in the afternoon. The tide out, we crunched through the pebbles and shells along the shore line. The air was heavy with the smell of the salt marshes and drying seaweed. I popped seaweed blisters and scaled flat pebbles out over the water. West counted the skips for me until the pebble gave up and sank to the bottom. Farther along, Grandpa Freudiger pried open a mussel shell with his pen knife. Everyone gasped as he tilted his head back and downed the oozing mess. Soon the sun dipped low in the sky. We looped back along the beach path and climbed the hill to the house.

The final stage of the holiday saw the family at table once more. The food-stained cloth had been cleared of the remnants of the great meal consumed a few hours before. A pot of tea rested in its place. Cups and saucers spread themselves out informally near a pile of teaspoons. There were bowls of walnuts and plates of dates and raisins and butter cookies. Missy, who never joined us in beach walks, prodded us to help ourselves, not to stand on ceremony. The conversation drifted to family matters: Aunt Clara was leaving Jersey for California. She was going to live with Clint and Edna in Santa Barbara. Her eyesight was failing, don't you know . . . Eddie wrote. He's still in Chicago. Says he's going into partnership with another man, a heating appliance business. So it went until my father pulled out his watch and announced they'd better get started. It was getting late and it was a long, cold drive back to the city. (There were no heaters in cars in those years.)

The thank-yous and goodbyes spilled from inside the house out into the driveway. There were hugs and kisses and handshakes and waves until everybody got settled into the Buick and the car rug in the back seat was in place over the laps of the passengers. My father stepped on the starter button and ran the engine up until it warmed. Voices rose in intensity with messages of goodbyes and say hellos to so-and-so when you see them. Arms waved from the car window as the car rolled back out of the driveway, stopped then pointed its headlights up the hill. It picked up a little speed, made the turn at the head of the hill and was gone. And it mattered not in the least to me that I was to be left with Missy for the next five days.

That first night was luxurious in its simplicity and lack of regimen. It might be spent in a game of dominos or checkers or lotto. Maybe West would show me how to operate the new radio. Even though radio reception was poor out here in the country, we fiddled with the wooden knobs of the new superheterodyne Stromberg-Carlson inside the doors of the oak-carved cabinet. Turning past the squeals and whistles, we searched the entire broadcast band. For a few minutes we listened to Joe Penner until the station faded out. We found a dance band for a while, but the music bent away so badly we gave up. West explained that it was a bad night for reception. The air layer was low, too much skip. It meant nothing to me.

The weight of the night closed in on us. We were tired and needed to go to bed. The yellow glow of the floor lamps added warmth to the chilly bedrooms. Missy closed the glass-paned doors to the great studio room shutting out the cold that had crept in after the fire had died away. She showed me my narrow, single bed. It was turned down to reveal coarse muslin sheets and layers of blankets and quilting. By the bed was a nighttable with a small reading lamp and a book. I undressed, pulled on my cotton flannel pajamas and slipped under the covers feeling their weight on me and the chill of my feet. I reached for my book as Missy left. This time the story was about a Tahitian boy who had climbed to the top of the tallest palm tree on his island, weighed it down and then arched it up into the sky. I stared sleepily in wonder at the color picture accompanying the text. Then the book was no longer in my hands. The top quilt came up over my head and my arms warmed. I drifted into a sea of blackness without dimensions. Then suddenly I was at the top of a great palm tree being lifted higher and higher into the air.

The grey light of the new day poked its way in through the bedroom window. Missy was standing by my bed in her holey, wool sweater and floor-length nightgown. "Awake yet? Cold this morning. We'll have to see about some heat," she croaked hoarsely. I listened for the clatter of her slippers down the cellar stairs, then heard the grinding as she rocked the burnt ashes out of the stove's grating. A shovel scraped the floor of the coal bin then rang as hit the side of the stove, its contents slipping into the furnace. The sound was repeated. I began to smell the coal gas, and pushed my way out of the envelope of blankets and heard Missy coughing her way back upstairs. Pulling my clothes from the chair, I headed for the register in the hall. The new heat drifted up through the squares of the polished cast iron register. I held my clothes out, article by article over the warm air and finally got dressed.

The kitchen was warm too now. Missy had turned on the gas in the oven and opened the door. West was already there absorbed in a book, a long ash from his cigarette dangling dangerously over his coffee. Taking the Ford, he would be on his way to the City this morning, Had to see an editor about illustrating a school edition of the Tales of Robin Hood . . . would be at the 14th Street apartment for several days . . . wasn't sure when he'd be back. Missy filled a bowl with steaming, gluelike oatmeal, set it out for me with the cream from the top of the milk bottle and said nothing. So Missy and I were to be left by ourselves for five days. Well, that was all right with me. Maybe I sensed that there was something wrong between Missy and West. But it didn't make any difference to me.

There are people born into this world for whom time has no meaning. Even as they grow old, they respond only to calls that come from deep inside themselves. Their actions are never swift, but rather measured and in answer to some need that has just surfaced. If they sense hunger, they eat. If they get tired, they sleep. And if they want to do something, they do it. They don't think about it. And they are never bothered about what other people might think of them. Missy was like that by nature. Untrammeled.

And if anyone was fool enough to call out to Missy, "Hurry up or we'll be late," he or she could almost be sure that they would be. Missy'd suddenly find something wrong about the way she was dressed, or forget where she put a letter she'd been wanting to mail. She'd flutter and she'd putter. Repeating all the while, "I'm coming . . . I'm coming . . ." But of course she wasn't.

Missy, too, was given to blurting out her thoughts exactly as they came to her regardless of where she was or who was with her. As the story goes, the summer Grandma Freudiger died the funeral service was held in the parlor of the Freudiger house in

Lincoln Park. The entire family was gathered there including Missy. It was hot and the service was long. At one point, Missy leaned over to say to my father, "I hope this is over soon," then to my mother, "We've got to get back to the Boathouse . . . It's our busy season, you know." My mother, who always had an acute sense of how to respond to an affront, bent over the casket and fairly yelled: "Did you hear that, Ma? You had some nerve dying now. Couldn't you have waited? Didn't you know that this was our busy season?" Missy remained sublimely unruffled by the rebuke while my mother went on to stiffle her sobs in her handkerchief.

I suppose if I had been the sort of child who had to be ministered to constantly those days at the Huntington Beach house would have been unendurable for both Missy and me. But as it was, I slipped easily away from the rigors of my home life and into Missy's careless way of disposing of time which was to dismiss all notions of what had to be done for what seemed like a good thing to do now. Whether she felt like walking down to Pokorny's little store by the beach for groceries or walking further by the water's edge to Centerport where we could get a malted milk, I went along happily. Each new day offered something new and exciting. We enjoyed one another's company and never got on one another's nerves, and the days passed quickly. And so did the years.

By the time I brought my new Iver Johnson twenty-eight inch "wheel," as Missy called my bicycle, from the Boathouse to ride the back hills of Huntington Beach, West was not there. I didn't know it at the time, but he had left for good.

30| Mrs. Barnes

MY MOTHER'S AUNT, Anna Rogers, was a practical nurse. She used to go off on "cases," geriatric cases where she lived in. I had always heard that she made pretty good money and that she preferred geriatric cases to pediatric cases. According to her, they were a lot easier.

Anna, even though she was my mother's aunt by some remote step relationship that I could never get clear, was only a year or so older than my mother. The two young women formed a strong bond soon after Anna emigrated from Germany just before the first world war.

Anna, née Glastetter, got past the greenhorn stage and learned English quickly, although she never lost her German accent. She was a jolly sort of person who loved to laugh. At some point she married a man by the name of Rogers, a South American whom her elder sister Paulina always referred to with contempt as a "nigger." It was rumored in the family that Anna contributed unstintingly to her husband's support and that he promptly gambled the money away. He was seen less and less of and finally, not at all. The marriage was short lived, the divorce imminent and uncontested. In fact, there was no one around to contest it.

Anna's life was far from ruined by the unhappy circumstances of her marriage. She and Paulina had put enough money away to buy and to settle nicely into a comfortable two-story frame house in Mountain View, New Jersey with their three German Shepherd dogs. My memories of having spent several days with the sisters off and on at a tender age fix on the large male dog they called Baron. At three or four, I was small enough and he was large enough for me to be able to ride around on his back. And that kept me busy and happy for hours. The great police dog never seemed to mind how I tugged and pulled at him. But I see I am drifting away from the particulars related to the matter of my account.

I was maybe seven or eight years old when my mother decided to take our old Buick sedan and drive over to Connecticut to visit Anna. Anna at this time was living in the house of and seeing to the needs of a ninety-two year old woman by the name of Mrs. Barnes. And Mrs. Barnes, Anna said, welcomed visitors.

It was not unusual for my mother to take me along on such trips. It was a relatively long drive then from Inwood-on-the-Hudson where we lived to Connecticut. My mother suggested that I might go with her. That meant that I was going. Admittedly, I wasn't the best company for this kind of a trip, but in fact the only company. My father's situation required that he look after his business on Sundays. It could be that Anna suggested bringing me, I don't recall. But I am sure that I didn't particularly want to go. I would rather have been playing with the kids along Payson Avenue and ranging the familiar heights of Inwood Hill Park.

The Buick crossed the 207th Street Bridge into the Bronx and headed up to University Heights. Following the network of trolley tracks to Gun Hill Road, then White Plains Road, we eventually got to the lower eastern regions of Westchester County. Crossing the state line into Connecticut somewhere above Greenwich, my mother wound the car around the curving roads that Anna's directions called for. We finally found John's Lane and the old salt box farm house.

Today the house would have had its portico decorated with a spread eagle and a plaque with bold numbers telling every passing motorist that it was built in 1746 and that its occupants had one way or another acquired the status of Connecticut Yankees.

At the time our car pulled into the cowpath alongside it, it was just another old farm house.

"My Gott," laughed Anna in her white uniform, "I wasn't sure you find the place!" She led the way, "So, come in . . . How are you, Dickie?" She looked down at me and could see that I was restless already. We went from the parlor where Anna took our coats, and on into the living room.

The living room was spacious. The wide old floorboards of uneven width were covered with a great oval hook rug. The room was dominated by a fireplace around which were arranged on the hook rug two cushioned chairs: one an armchair, the other a rocker. There was in addition a straight-backed chair between the other two chairs. Above the mantel of the fireplace hung a fowling piece of uncertain age. And opposite the fireplace across the room from it was a carpeted staircase that turned suddenly as it was about to reach the second floor of the house. Anna's "case" was nowhere to be seen, nor was there any evidence of her occupancy.

I sat down in the rocker and immediately began to test its limits. "Mrs. Barnes takes her afternoon nap now," announced Anna. "She gets up in a little while . . . So, how haf you been, Emmy?" The question was anticipated. There was no direct answer, but it was a signal for the two women to exchange bits of family news. I grew more restless and bored than ever, wishing that I had put up some kind of fight to get out of this adult world of affairs. "Here, Dickie," said Anna, "I get you some cookies." She got up from the straight-backed chair reserved for her station and swept off into another room that could only have been the kitchen. Before my mother could say "sit still," the thumping began.

It came from somewhere just above our heads. It was not a frantic kind of thump, but rather a steady beating that came on for a few seconds, then left off. Anna whisked back into the living room. "Mrs. Barnes. I go get her . . . Come on, we all sit in the kitchen." She showed us the way into the other room, then turned back and headed for the stairs.

The kitchen was spacious. It was white and dishes and cups of varying sizes were encased in the windowed cupboards along opposing walls. There was a cast iron stove of another time, still in use, set near the end of one wall and a large oilcloth covered table in the middle of the room. Around it were solid looking yellow-stained oak chairs. The lingering smell of oatmeal hovered about the room.

My mother and I sat at the table and waited. There was that dreaded moment of anticipation where I was going to meet some shrunken old woman who was about to enter my life then exit it just as quickly, leaving me with exactly nothing. The situation was suddenly intolerable. The more so because I consented to it. I was angry, but most of all with myself.

We listened to the clopping on the stairs, ker-bump, ker-bump.

Then it stopped telling us that the stairs had been fully negotiated. We heard Anna saying, "So, come. We go in the kitchen." Anna and the old woman appeared. She held the woman's arm firmly. They advanced slowly to the table. "Mrs. Barnes, there is my niece, Emmy and her son, Dickie." My mother stood up and gestured for me to do the same. The old woman put her free hand on the table and looked down to be sure her feet were firmly planted. Her white hair was pulled back into a bun. At last she lifted herself up straight. She wore a simple blue cotton print dress bordered at the neck and sleeves with white lace. She looked around. Her eyes searched and at last found the strangers in her midst. She worked her mouth into a smile and offered her skeletal hand, first to my mother then to me.

I didn't get it all at first. All I knew was that I was suddenly released from the tension that had built up inside me. There was something about the face, the mouth, particularly the eyes of this old woman that now looked directly at me as she said, her throat not yet fully cleared for speaking, "Why, I'm very glad to know you." I was somehow certain she was.

The frail little woman sipped at her tea as did my mother. Anna rustled about in the kitchen from sink to ice box to table. I soaked my cookies in my glass of milk until they broke off and I had to spoon the soggy mess up along the side of the glass. For once my mother seemed at a loss for words, even to advise me of this breach of etiquette.

I thought about the one meeting I had had with my great-grandmother. Other than this, I really didn't know much about old people, especially those who had reached a great age. But now I found myself quite taken with Mrs. Barnes who now with trembling hand, yet practiced assurance set her cup back into its saucer and folded her hands on the table. "We don't have many visitors," she said. I realized the remark was clearly directed to me. Her red-rimmed eyes sparkled as she spoke and I had a sudden knowledge of a bond that was beginning to build between us. A moment ago I was wrestling with the thought of how I was going to entertain myself for the next two hours or so in this dreary setting. Now here I was completely taken in by this old woman who had nothing to offer me in the usual sense of what I needed to hold my attention. "Have you seen my garden?" she asked. No, I had not. "Well then, if Anna will help me, I think we can go outside while it's still light and you can see some of my plants. Do you think you would like that?" Normally it would be the last thing in the world I would like, yet here I found myself nodding an almost enthusiastic yes.

It was a late September day. The sun was low and the air was crisp and clear and thick with the smell of drying leaves. Mrs. Barnes held her cane in one hand while Anna supported her by the other arm. The weeds had begun to overgrow the crooked kitchen garden gate behind the house. "Herbs," said Mrs. Barnes, "That's all I grow now. They're hardy." She lifted her cane and pointed. "Coriander. Pull the seeds and smell." I loosened a few beads from a spray and rolled them around between my fingers.

I put them to my nose and made a face. Mrs. Barnes gave out with a little laugh.

We went further down among the little beds. I sampled the drying tarragon leaves, the English thyme and finally the sage leaves which left a pungent odor on my fingers. "I've always liked herbs the best," said Mrs. Barnes. "They last when the tomatoes and beans are all gone and their vines have all dried up." The sun dipped behind a tree and a shadow fell across the little garden. There was a sudden chill in the air. "We go in now," said Anna.

Mrs. Barnes sat in her favorite chair in the living room facing the fireplace. I sat across from her in the rocker, for once not trying to see how far back it would go. Anna and my mother were in the kitchen discussing the health of Paulina. "Come closer, can you?" said Mrs. Barnes. She looked tired now. I walked the rocker over to where I could see her face. "Give me your hand," she said. I felt the gnarled old bones of her fingers shift under my grip. "You are a kind boy to have come all this way to see me," She looked directly at me. The small centers of her tired eyes gave off a light of their own. The surrounding features bore no sign of strain. Her lips trembled as she made a little smile. I looked back at her and across the centuries. "You have brought me a lot of happiness today," said the ancient woman closing her other hand over mine, then gently patting it.

I was quiet and didn't fidget on the long ride back to New York. My mother said finally, "Are you feeling all right? You're not going to be sick, are you?" "No," I replied simply. I couldn't bring myself to talk about what had passed between the old lady and me, so I didn't try. Actually, I was having some trouble trying to figure it out for myself. My mother kept turning her eyes away from the road to look down at me, squinting, trying to find some sign of what ailed me. She finally let it go with a grimace and a humph.

A week later we learned from Anna that Mrs. Barnes had died. Anna was back in Mountain View with Paulina taking a few days rest and looking for a new "case." Death was beyond my beyond my comprehension at that time, so Mrs. Barnes's passing did not particularly trouble me. The announcement came like any other bit of news and was no more nor less noteworthy. In fact, I don't think I ever really considered the impact of that fleeting encounter with Mrs. Barnes of so many years ago. I never discussed it with anyone. I couldn't have put it into words anyway. I was a boy, and a boy understands that special kind of meeting only intuitively. He cannot say what it means at the time it happens and so puts it in the back of his mind. Something happened. That was all.

The Author about 1934

31| Georgie 1

GEORGIE SCHULZ WAS a spindly little blond-haired kid with a squeaky voice that came from somewhere in the back of his throat. We came to know one another at P.S. 52, in the Friday afternoon club period. We were both interested in stamp collecting, so we opted for the Stamp Club.

Mrs. MacGowan was a kindly old primary grades school teacher who regularly specialized in art. Aside from her interest in children, stamps would have been the kind of thing that attracted her—probably because of the endless variety of designs and colors.

At any rate, she was quite knowledgeable and showed us the difference between perforate and imperforate, and flat plate and rotary press stamps. She showed us surcharged stamps and precancelled U.S. stamps with city and state names in bars across them. She encouraged us to send away for unusual stamp covers which she must have read about. Georgie and I decided to write to some remote island in the Samoan group in the South Pacific for the "Tin-can Canoe" stamp.

Georgie's mother and father lived in a small apartment in a three-story tenement built among those early buildings as Inwood's populations grew. The building was located on a tiny, numbered cross streets along the Harlem flats issuing from Tenth Avenue. As I remember, it was 203rd Street. Learning that Georgie's father was a stamp collecter, I began to spend those gray fall Saturday afternoons under the single lamp hanging from the living room ceiling over the stamp-cluttered card table.

Georgie's father was a thick-set man with heavy jowls and a brush haircut. He wore black pants and a white athletic undershirt. He peered through wire glasses and muttered in a heavy German accent as he puffed on his pipe and sorted stamps with his flat-bladed tweezers. "Dis series, impoiforate, iss walubul . . . Dis here . . . nodding." He pulled out stamps with the imperial German eagle printed on them, then began to arrange crowned war maiden stamps by denomination. He pointed to piles of surcharged stamps where the denominations had been raised, in some cases from five marks to 800,000. "Dese var von der tventies, shust after der var . . . Invlation. It vas toirible." He had von Hindenburg heads in every imaginable color and denomination, some of them black-bordered to mark the death of the old statesman. We were sorting stamps at a time not long after Adolph Hitler had come to power as chancellor of Germany. That seemed not to bother anybody here—certainly not stamp collectors.

These Saturday afternoons were long and pleasant. They usually ended when Georgie's mother came into the living room with a trayful of stollen and cookies, a glass of milk for Georgie and me, and a pot of tea for Mr. Schulz. She was a thin, bony-faced woman with greying hair swept back to a bun at the nape of her neck. She wore an apron, and I hadn't been aware that she was in the apartment until that moment.

It was through these little milk and tea breaks when Georgie's mother joined us that I learned that Georgie was about to be confirmed as a Lutheran. Church was a thing that hadn't concerned me until this moment. Suddenly I had the feeling that I was missing out on something. I went home with questions on my mind. I approached my mother and father about this business of religion. I knew that my mother was raised as a Catholic (I saw the rosary beads passed on to her by her mother) though she never went to church. She shied away at the mention of the religion. My father was a disinterested protestant by baptism and by heritage, if not by choice. "That's entirely up to you," he said flattening out his voice as he always did when it came to a discussion of serious matters. I mentioned that Georgie was about to become a member of his church. Maybe I'd like to do that too. "We won't interfere with any decision you make for yourself about religion . . . whatever religion you choose." Well if no one cared, then I'd become a Lutheran.

The Lutheran Church on Post Avenue was dark and cold. The unsmiling, bespectacled pastor handed me my catechisms and told me to memorize a section of them by the following Thursday afternoon. He would hear me then. I came back a week later with memorized answers to the questions he asked. I got them right, but they didn't make much sense to me. I continued regularly Thursday afternoons after school for the next four weeks. There was no Sunday school at this church, and maybe I went once or twice to the Sunday worship service with Georgie and his family, I don't remember. In any event, the whole thing suddenly appeared to me a rather bleak prospect. One Thursday afternoon I didn't return for my catechism recitations. Lutheranism, as I saw it, was not for me. I never went back to that church.

32| Alex

THE KATZENBERGS LIVED in an apartment in 1 Payson, above their tailor shop on Dyckman Street. They were a father, a mother and three boys, Izzy, Manny and Alex. They all worked in the shop: Mrs. Katzenberg, a redheaded woman who handstitched by the plate glass window from morning till night; Mr. Katzenberg, a wiry little man in an athletic undershirt, balding at the temples who cut, worked over the machine and pressed suits; the boys who ran the finished garments on wire hangers draped over their backs to customers' apartments.

The Katzenbergs were busy people, always at work and always angry—or so it seemed to me. They were very matter of fact and never laughed. Even their dog Whitey wouldn't take time out to play. He'd slip out from under any well-meaning hand that tried to pet him and trot away rudely. Except for business, mother and father Katzenberg wanted nothing to do with kids. And you had better not get in their way. Alex, the youngest of three sons, was the only one who was different, and then only when he was away from the family.

Alex Katzenberg and I were placed in the same class at P.S. 52 from the 1st to the 5th grade. He had straight blond hair that hung forward over his eyes. (Izzy had his father's black hair that ran backwards on his head. Manny had his mother's crop of blazing red hair.) And where Izzy and Manny were normal-sized, compactly built, quick, and sharp-witted, Alex was small, slow and sluggish. He had an annoying habit of pushing his face into yours when he spoke, breathing on you—and his breath reeked. It was as if he'd been eating a fish, onion and sour cream concoction that hadn't really digested. On the other hand, his teeth may have been at the core of the problem. While they were perfectly even and looked good and strong, they were tinged with a kind of green moss suggesting that he rarely, if ever brushed them.

Alex was a physical kid too. He liked to grab you and hold onto you and pull at you while he talked to you, polluting you with his foul breath. Maybe he thought it was the only way he could get your attention. On the other hand, he might have sensed that this grabbing and pulling would annoy you and did it out of a kind of perversity. Anyway, his habit used to put me off, so I tried to avoid Alex as much as I could.

One time coming out of the park by Bolton Road onto Payson Avenue, I reached down absently to pick up the remains of a broomhandle, probably once used when whole as a stickball bat. I was with Ole and didn't even notice that Alex was behind me watching. Alex suddenly grabbed my arm, "Hey, that's mine . . ." He reached for the stick. I shook him off and walked away. He came after me and pulled at my jacket again. Again, "Hey . . ." I wheeled and hit him in the mouth. He went down and looked up at me stunned. He didn't cry. He just looked surprised.

But Alex would have his moment too. A month or two later, at midday we were scuffing our way along Dyckman Street on our way home from school for lunch. We waited for the big, silver-haired Irish cop with the 34 on his tunic lapel to send us across the dangerous Broadway-Riverside Drive intersection. Alex began his grabbing and pulling. I twisted away and he hit me square in the gut, knocking the wind out of me. I doubled up. Alex's mouth dropped open. He held onto me.

"Jeez, I'm sorry. Are you hurt? I didn't mean to . . . You okay?" I kept fighting for air. Alex was relieved when I finally straightened up. He looked genuinely distressed, but watched my face all the while. "S'okay . . ." I finally managed. I took it he hadn't meant to hurt me, that he hit me harder in the right place than he wanted to, and that his apology was genuine.

Could I have had him wrong all this time? I never did find out. We soon drifted apart, each into our own separate worlds.

33| Claude

THE ROLLANDS SOLD their New Rochelle house and moved to a three-story, two-family brownstone on Congress Street in Brooklyn. Evelyn's father had died leaving her mother alone to care for the big Brooklyn house. The family, now larger by Paul, Jr. felt that it made sense to move in with her. The ongoing depression, too, was a factor. It was agreed that the Rollands should keep the lower two floors for themselves while renting out the third floor to a small family as an apartment.

With the subway to connect us now, I could see Claude more often and on each of our visits we renewed our friendship by showing each other some new trick, invention or game we had learned since we last saw one another.

If Evelyn Rolland was a loud, vigorous and commanding presence in the life of young Claude, his father was just the opposite. Paul Rolland, Sr. was thoughtful and quiet. He was a gaunt man with a great hawk nose, ever with a long cigar encircled in his lips. He never said much, either because he was reluctant to take the cigar out of his mouth, or because he really didn't have that much to say. And he never talked about his work.

My mother and father were never sure what Paul Rolland did for a living. Rumor had it that he was a "scout" for Walter Winchell, and that he hung around New York's plush watering holes soaking up gossip. The theory was plausible enough because he was quiet and attentive and people would confide in him. No matter. We boys loved to be around him because he thought like a boy and

knew what we liked and always had something new to show us.
And Claude, like his father, spoke little, preferring to communicate
by body language.

I was probably no more than seven when I was first allowed
to go by myself to Brooklyn on the subway to visit Claude. The
afternoon usually began with a tour of the streets. Claude, who
was then going to the Friends school, led me around the
neighborhood and introduced me to his friends as they turned
up, advising me that they never had anything to do with the
scorned Syrians. Later, we might choose up sides for a "fistball"
game, which rivaled our P.S. 52 punchball game in interest and
intensity because of the added pitcher.

Evenings at the Rollands were passed in progressive stages
of family activity, each of which had been formalized and had
some purposeful place in the Rolland household's scheme of
things. This deliberateness was probably guided by the prominent
presence of "Gog," Evelyn's mother. (Claude's name for his
grandmother, like my "Missy," was almost certainly an early
attempt to vocalize Grandma.) At any rate Gog, nothing at all like
her daughter, was always very much in control of the situation.
Her soft-spoken "Now, Claude . . . " was more of an appeal than
a threat. Still, she meant it and Claude never tried his disappearing
act with her.

Even the simple business of washing up before dinner took
on special significance before Gog: hands washed up to the elbows
and fingernails clean. When the dinner was ready, Gog called us
all to table and directed us where to sit. The food was passed
with great ceremony as if each platter had been precisely
measured for the amount of food required for family and guest
consumption. We ate and asked to be excused, retiring to the
spacious living room past the great rolling pocket doors. Paul,
Sr. soon joined us and we folded the legs of a card table out and
set it up adding chairs. The game was poker. Claude and his dad
were proficient at it and they taught me quickly how to play.
Later came the drinks. Gog interrupted at exactly the right moment

with a trayful of glasses brimming with ginger ale. It was a new drink for me and it had a bite that I wasn't used to. I sipped at it and signalled that I approved, in as grown up a way as I could manage. A few more hands and the game was over and it was time for us boys to go to bed. Gog showed me to a corner sofa prepared for me. The sheets had been neatly turned back. We exchanged handshakes and good nights. Every stage of decorum was observed right to the end.

It was fortunate for me, too, that the Rollands had a cottage on Fire Island and that my mother and I were invited to spend a few days there each summer. It was a long trip for us, but one that I looked forward to eagerly. Unless we went by car, traveling to Fire Island usually meant that we had to take the Long Island Railroad to Babylon and wait there while the electric locomotive was changed for a steam-powered one for the train to continue its run to Montauk at the end of Long Island—even though the very next stop, Bayshore, was ours.

The ferry to Ocean Beach left the Maple Avenue docks on a regular schedule and we usually had time for a sandwich and a malted milk at the corner drug store and luncheonette on Bayshore's Main Street before taking the short taxi ride to the docks. The ferry was a large, lumbering tub that chugged its way slowly and monotonously across Great South Bay. It worked its way through the channels toward the four prominent chimneys of the new community house, docking at Ocean Beach. Ocean Beach was the largest summer community on the thin spit of land known as Fire Island which ran ninety miles along the south shore of Long Island separating the Atlantic Ocean from the shallow, protected waters of Great South Bay. People, then as now, waited on the docks for arriving family and friends with wagons. There were no cars on Fire Island.

The Rolland cottage had been in the family since 1917 and was one of the first to be built on Wilmot Road, then a simple boardwalk raised up over the sand crossing the half-mile width of the island from bay to ocean. There was little by way of amenities here or elsewhere at that time on Fire Island. The cottage was a crude woodframe shell with small, back bedrooms and a screened-in front porch. The floors were worn smooth from the sand of years that you somehow could never get off your feet. Outside the cottage there was a long-armed hand pump for water. Inside, there were kerosene lamps for light at night. Cooking was accomplished over a simple, bottled gas camp stove, and food and ice were wagoned in in small quantities from the village store.

If you were a child totally lacking in imagination, one who had to be stimulated constantly, Fire Island would still be a boy-heaven where you could never be bored. Within minutes of arriving at the cottage, I was out of my street clothes and into my bathing suit. Claude and I took turns in the wagon, pulling one another, thumping over the spaces between the weathered boards. Our mothers gave up trying to keep up with us. The water was always warmer in the bay. It was also calmer. You could wade in from the beach and never have to worry about being knocked down by waves. Claude and I showed one another how we'd learned to dog paddle and to open our eyes under the water. We took the afternoon to get reacquainted in this new environment, one we both loved.

Back at the cottage Claude and I had time before supper to look around. Claude led me to the back bedrooms and showed me the cot next to a wall where I'd be sleeping. He pointed to a knot hole and then led me around to his bedroom. There, by his bed was the knothole. This meant that we could communicate secretly with one another at night, passing notes, shells and other objects through the hole until we were drowsy enough to fall asleep.

The next morning we were out right after breakfast thumping the boardwalks with the wagon. Claude brought me around to the back of a large cottage that wasn't occupied. He pulled the dense foliage back away from the siding, opened the lattice work, and we slipped through and under the house. It was a hiding place. In the shadows there, half-buried in the sand was a cigar box. Claude opened it and showed me his collection of baseball cards, lead soldiers and the three dollars and twenty-five cents in coins he had saved. He swore me to secrecy and from his pocket added another fifteen cents to his bank. We organized the soldiers into lines of battle and moved them against one another like chess pieces. As one after the other fell, the battle came to an end and we climbed out into the sun, blinking.

Claude had the habit of slipping the seed stalks out of the long grasses along the boardwalk and chewing on them. He either worked them into his mouth like cat whiskers, or let them hang down with the seed sprays dangling in the air. It was one of his tricks that I picked up quickly. He was also heedless of the poison ivy that grew in abundance with the other island vegetation, because he was immune to it. Unhappily, I was not. A few days after our first visit to Ocean Beach, my face puffed up and my eyes closed. My arms and legs were streaked with lines of itching blisters. It took a doctor's injection to quiet the raging infection. In years to come I was more cautious. Claude used to laugh at me when I backed away from the shiny, three-leaf plants that ranged along the sides of the boardwalks. He demonstrated the extent of his immunity by tearing off a handful of the leaves, stuffing them in his mouth, chewing and swallowing them.

No trip to Fire Island was ever complete without a day on the ocean side of Fire Island. We usually reserved my last day on the island for this. The fine white sand beach was wide and unbroken in its length as far as the eye could see. There were beach umbrellas scattered here and there and, silhouetted against the sky, the Ocean Beach water tower. Couples passed one another walking hand in hand at the water's edge where smaller children played giddily trying to stay ahead of each incoming wave.

The ocean at Fire Island was always acknowledged to be treacherous. If there was a heavy surf running, even a strong swimmer was powerless against the force of the waves. At waist depth he suddenly found that he couldn't move. The undertow was strong. There was no way to avoid the relentless walls of water surging in at the swimmer and falling on him, twisting, turning and pounding his body into the sand where the undertow gripped him Even on calmer days, an unwary swimmer might fall victim to the "sea puss" or run-out and panic when he discovered he was too far out and found it impossible to swim back to shore.

It was always a happier time at the beach for Claude and me when Paul Rolland was on hand. Our mothers bellowed after us if we ventured out into the ocean beyond knee-depth. But if Paul, Sr. was with us, it was another matter. We'd be learning how to respect the waves, how to watch them and manage them so that we could get more fun out of our surf swimming.

I wasn't really sure what porpoises did in the ocean, but Paul demonstrated how we had to dive into the waves just like they did, dip under the wave just as it began to curl over us and come up in the trough on the other side. Next he showed us how to ride a wave in. You had to stand in waist deep water, at exactly the point where the waves were breaking. When the right wave came along, one with a good high swell, you kicked off, lifted your head and rode before the curl as far into shore as the wave would take you. We practiced long until we got it right. The ocean became a friendly place for us now, some of its wildness tamed to our uses.

The trips to Fire Island continued from year to year and Claude always had some new game or some new bit of perversity to color our days together.

By the time we were ten years old, our mothers felt that we were old enough to profit from a tour of the nation's capital—a mistake. We'd be going in the Rollands' new Ford V-8 sedan. It would be more comfortable to enjoy the ride in the new car. We kids would be contained, which certainly would not be the case if we went by rail. It was unusually warm weather we were enjoying that Easter season. There was the promise that the Japanese cherry trees would be in bloom. But Evelyn Rolland should have known better the moment she saw Claude spit through his teeth for the first time.

Now, a normal ten year old boy is not troubled to find ways to make his surroundings compatible and bend them entirely to his uses. Put two of them together and you will witness improvisational skills at their most creative. It was the year I had come up with the miniature sling shot. You loaded the missile in folded hands with a stone not much larger than a grain of sand You aimed quickly and let fly. The tiny Y-shaped sling shot then folded quickly and neatly into the palm of your hand. It happened so fast that detection was near to impossible. Even if someone saw something, he couldn't be sure what it was. This was our entertainment on the way to Washington. From the back seat of the Ford, unnoticed, we took turns pinging away at autos going in the opposite direction, probably starring a few windshields. By the time we reached Washington's outskirts and found a tourist home, we knew that this trip held out real promise for our resourceful skills.

That night we had supper in a restaurant nearby. Claude pulled one of two straws out of its protective sheath for his milk and shot a glance over at me. I watched him tear off a bit of the thin paper and work it into a ball between his thumb and forefinger. He moved the ball to his mouth for a fraction of a second, then into the straw. The two mothers were deep in conversation, too busy to notice. Claude aimed the straw at the kid at the next table and let go. By the time the kid pulled the tiny wad off the back of his neck and looked around, Claude had the straw in his milk. Our eyes met once again as I loaded my straw. So much for dead time at the dinner table.

My guess was that Claude had noticed the ballplayers at Ebbet's Field spitting through their teeth. Baseball is a traditional game that is rich in stlylistic gestures and mannerisms. Spitting, virtually unheard of in other sports, is a part of baseball and perfectly acceptable. Even desirable—if it's done right: a turn of the head and a quick release of a thin line of juice (then tobacco) into the dirt. Claude had it down pat and I soon learned it. Walking the gardens of Mount Vernon wasn't at all boring for us Every fresh bloom was a target. By the time we got to the top of the Washington Monument, we'd settled the rules for a contest to see who could spit the farthest.

Claude, too, had many opportunities to do his disappearing act in Washington. One scolding from his mother and he was gone, invisible for over an hour. I knew where he was that morning we visited the Smithsonian Institute, but I wasn't going to say. Later, in the Treasury Building one of the guards returned him to his embarrassed mother.

The Washington trip was a kind of high water mark for Claude and me as boys. As our adolescent years approached we drifted apart. I got involved with the Boy Scouts and later with the Mount Washington church's activities. Claude went on to Boys High and got to be a pretty fair ball player. The few times we saw one another then, it was to play some sand lot ball. And that was usually in Inwood when he'd come to visit me and stay over. Or, on winter Saturdays, I might subway to Brooklyn. We'd go ice skating in Prospect Park. At times when Paul, Sr. had tickets, we'd go to a hockey game at Madison Square Garden. We spoke to one another more like adults now, and it was clear that our carefree boyhood years were gradually slipping away from us. At last we saw one another not at all—that is, until after the war.

34| Georgie 2

MY NEXT ASSOCIATION with Georgie was with the VFW
Fort Tryon Post 3037's newly organized fife, drum and bugle corps.
The idea was Mr. Collins's. He was a wiry little man with a shock
of white hair, missing front teeth and a New York dialect that was
born and nursed along somewhere in Hell's Kitchen. Other drum
and bugle corps were being organized by VFW and American
Legion posts throughout the City. Why shouldn't Inwood's veterans
be represented?

The first organizational meeting took place in Mr. Collins's
apartment on Dyckman Street in one of those old buildings that
rear-ended on P.S. 52's school yard. Georgie and I had heard
about it in school. Planning to enlist as buglers, we found ourselves in the living room waiting for Mr. Collins to speak. The
room was crowded with boys and the meeting was brief.
"Rehoisals'll begin nex' week . . . Thoisday at P.S. fi'ty two . . .
Da groun' flaw by da Boys ent-rance, se'em a'clock. Be dere on
time. If yer a bugla an' ya got a bugle, bring it witcha. Fa youse
drummas, we got some drums. All yez'l need is da sticks."

The small asphalt-floored Boys inner yard with its one basketball
backboard was alive with noise. A drum coach was trying to teach a
handful of boys in a circle around him a 6/8 marching cadence;
buglers blatted away trying to learn "You're in the Army Now." The
fife players had isolated themselves in a remote corner by the stairwell
trying to get the hang of a scale on their six-holed wooden fifes.
Georgie and I were giddy with the excitement of the moment and the
prospects of lining up to march in a parade.

We learned our five-note march adaptations and our drum beats rapidly, and with the better weather, we were learning our formations in P. S. 52's schoolyard outdoors. Our first public appearance came at the Decoration Day Parade along Dyckman Street from the Dyckman Oval at Nagle Avenue to the Triangle at Broadway and Riverside Drive. We were told soon after that we were ready for uniforms and were pressed into selling books of raffle tickets to family, friends and neighbors.

Some weeks later the uniforms came. They were a gaudy light blue with darker blue collars and cuffs. The VFW maltese cross was sewn onto the left shoulder of a waist-length gabardine jacket. Gold letters were stitched onto an overseas cap, and Georgie and I quickly earned our corporal stripes and gold and silver bugling medals. It was our job now to teach new buglers the tunes and to rehearse the bugle section.

The Author, 1936

Our parades now included City-wide competitions at Manhattan Beach and Madison Square Garden. We had grown rapidly as a drum and bugle corps, and going on these outings was an exciting experience.

With the end of our first parade season, during which we had received honorable mention in some of the more important competitions, Mr. Collins decided that there should be a little celebration for us and our families upstairs at the K. of C. hall across from the IRT Subway Station at Nagle Avenue and Dyckman Street. There was beer and soft drinks and a small quartet consisting of a piano, violin, bass viol and drums to play for dancing. Round tables with paper coverings ringed the dance floor. My Uncle Ed, who was visiting from Chicago, an overseas veteran of the World War himself, made it a special family event for my family. Georgie was there too, with his mother and father. And there were girls our age, shy, showing one another how to dance.

A boy ten or eleven years old had a hard time then accepting girls at any level. Yet here the moment seemed to call for just that. "Why don't you ask that little girl, the pretty one over there, to dance with you?" prompted Uncle Ed. Georgie, who was standing by my side giggled from the back of his throat. "I don't know how to dance," I said, turning red. But there wasn't much else to do unless you just wanted to sit. But the thought of dancing made us silly. We tried a bit of it with one another, but ended up going goofy, skidding across the dance floor. The idea was totally new—dancing with a girl . . . I couldn't do that! I had to admit though, the girls looked and acted differently somehow. They were attractive in their party dresses and they smiled at us, those we knew from P.S. 52. They weren't their usual fresh-mouthed selves like they were in school.

Except for a few brief encounters in school, the boyhood experiences Georgie and I shared ended as unceremoniously as they began. We simply lost one another in the shuffle—probably when I quit the VFW Drum and Bugle corps to join the Boy Scouts' drum and bugle corps the following year.

35| Frank 1

FRANK WALD WAS small for his eleven years. He had curly black hair, cut short in the fashion of the times, and the many small locks drew naturally to his head. He never had to, so never did bother to part it. He was evenly dark-complexioned, except for his nose which didn't seem to belong to his face. Frank blew it constantly as if he couldn't get something out of it. And so his nose was always red, except for in winter when it went purple.

Frank spoke slowly and with a lazy drawl, measuring his words carefully. His vocabulary was advanced well beyond his years. He read easily anything and everything within range of his eyesight which almost surely contributed to a need for glasses by the time he was ready for junior high school. Words intrigued Frank, and so he found schoolboy vernacular amusing. He would seldom use it himself except in some context that would ridicule its naivete: "They call ya 'yel-lah' because ya won't hitch a ride onna backa the street car."

I met Frank when I had just turned twelve. We got to know one another in the great schoolyard, as kids generally do, without benefit of formal introduction. We struck up a casual converation one lunch hour while we were waiting for the bell to ring. We were awed by the newness of junior high school. How we now moved from room to room where there was a different teacher for each subject.

The great schoolyard of P.S., and lately, JHS 52, Manhattan which had been the garden of the old Ward School 52 some fifty years before, was the common meeting ground for school children at lunch hour. The yard was a vast field of concrete scored conveniently into three foot squares making it easy to chalk out bases and boundaries for an assortment of ball games. The big yard was bordered by a ten-foot high chain link fence that ran along Vermilyea Avenue. It began at the rear wall of the five-story apartment building that fronted on Dyckman Street (where Mr. Collins lived) and ended at the Academy Street school building. Inside the fence, and framed by the el of the school structure, there was a smaller yard reserved for the younger children during school hours. The fence gate was the entrance to the newly established junior high school.

The boys and girls who attended school here gathered rapidly in the great schoolyard at lunchtime. By 12:15, if the weather was good, the yard seethed with youngsters, some carrying rolled-up shop aprons, others schoolbooks strapped together with sneakers dangling by the laces. By ritual, the boys flopped their brown paper-covered books down on the concrete by the fence. They darted here and there chasing balls, laughing, taunting one another with the schoolboy insults they had learned. They raised their voices to provoke reactions or to reply to dares.

The girls were somewhat more constrained. They fell into little groups and whispered secrets to one another about the boys they admired, or those they couldn't stand.

In the far corner of the great yard there was a serious punchball game going on. A skilled hitter bent low and dropped the "spauldeen" from one hand. As it bounced back up from the pavement he caught it inside the fist of his other hand. The ball scudded between the shortstop and third baseman and rolled out to the left fielder. A double by the time it was returned to the infield. Then followed the inevitable shouting match: "He was safe! . . . He was out!"

By 12:30 new groups began to form at the gates. These were the children who regularly ate at home. The girls now spread out into larger groups and seemed to have a lot to say to one another, their conversations being animated by squeals of laughter. The boys, old confronting new, baited one another, pounded at one another, grappled with one another. With endless reserves of energy they tore at each another's coats, sweaters and button-flies, they played "saloojie" with an easy mark's woolen cap, they tripped one another up from behind. Then, in the heat of it all, from somewhere over the mêlée came a persistent clangor. The school's bells rang loud and long. It was the signal for order.

Slowly, hypnotically the children obeyed. They drifted into the alleyway by the junior high school's double-door entrance and formed into vague lines. Someone from inside the school opened the doors. Properly subdued, the children ambled through the cool, dark, crayon-smelling corridors to find their home rooms for the two-hour afternoon session.

Frank Wald was in 7B, a half-year ahead of me in the newly-created junior high. From his classes he soon got to know most of the Payson Avenue gang that lived along the block by Inwood Hill Park: Ole, Corelli, Fat, and Joey, my regular after-school companions. He volunteered that he preferred their company to those kids he knew from P.S. 98, from where he had just been transferred. These were the kids who mostly hung around his block at Sherman Avenue and 207th Street. "Schmucks," he called them, "Always trying to gyp you out of something or go you one better." I gathered it was a relief for him to have been moved to the junior high, even though most of these others he disliked soon followed after him. For his part, Frank felt that they were no longer of any consequence. He was only too glad to join up with kids who had something new and different to offer.

It wasn't long after our schoolyard introduction that Frank and I found ourselves in the gymnasium of yet another school one evening. It was the newer elementary school at Nagle Avenue and Ellwood Street. Troop 727, Manhattan of the Boy Scouts of America had begun to meet there every Thursday evening. Frank and I had talked about becoming Boy Scouts. Troop 727 had recently been created to serve the growing juvenile population of Inwood.

As scout troops went, 727 was a large and disorganized affair. Probably because it was new. But also because it had no affiliation with any church or civic organization. Little groups of brand new scouts and still newer recruits were scattered at various stations in the gym. Without warning some kid in corduroy knickers, stockings rolled down to his sneakers would jump up and bolt across the floor to visit with a school friend. Others simply shrieked out names, sending their high-pitched voices ricochetting off the hard-baked surfaces of the yellow block walls. They pulled themselves up ropes. They waved wig-wag flags. They swatted one-another with knotted clothes lines. They chased one another in and out of swinging doors and into the stairwells of the school. No one looked to be in charge of things here.

Frank and I craned forward wanting to hear. We sat cross-legged on the mirror-like hardwood floor trying to sort out our instructions from a junior assistant scoutmaster. We were assigned to something called the Fox Patrol, and a week later we recited the Scout Oath, Laws and Motto, tied our knots and officially became Tenderfoot Scouts.

By the time Frank and I were ready for further advancement we had transferred to Troop 757, the smaller, more disciplined troop housed in Mt. Washington Presbyterian Church which was also closer to where each of us lived. At my schoolmate Woodrow's urging I had begun Sunday school at Inwood's first, and therefore oldest church where I was already playing on the basketball team. I soon learned about the Scout troop sponsored by the church and asked Frank what he thought about transferring. I knew he was Jewish and wasn't sure if he wanted to hook up with a church-sponsored troop. He simply shrugged. "Shit. I don't care. If they don't."

Mapmaking was the troublesome requirement for advancing from Tenderfoot Scout to Second Class Scout. Most of the other candidates of 757 had sensibly limited their mapwork to a few, well chosen, square city blocks. Like so much schoolwork, I saw this as drudgery and not very challenging. So I proposed to Frank that we team up and map Inwood Hill Park.

Now, here were 167 acres of rugged, wooded hillsides and winding paths, all of which I knew intimately from having explored every cliff and cave since I was seven years old. Frank, who knew little of the Park, agreed. It did sound like more of an adventure, even though he usually preferred to do his assignments rapidly and with a minimum of effort.

I borrowed my uncle's brass, Army Engineer Corps compass, Frank turned pages to the back of an old school notebook and for four days we took bearings, paced off distances and recorded field notes. Finally we sat down and laid the whole thing out on paper.

The perimeter of the Park was defined by Dyckman Street on the south. By Payson, then Seaman Avenue on the east. On the west were the paths that ran inside the new ballparks along the Hudson. These lines were more or less straight. It was the path that began after the footbridge over the railroad tracks and into the park that made for the problem. It was long, hilly and winding. Tunneling under the new Henry Hudson Parkway, it rose and snaked northwards up to the Parkway bridge that crossed Spuyten Duyvil Creek. From there it dropped down again to follow the loop of the Creek, dividing the Inwood hills from the playgrounds of Farmers Field. Where the lines ought to have come together at Isham Street and Seaman Avenue to complete the circuit, on our map there was a gaping maw. If the lines had crossed or even pointed towards one another, we probably could have found errors in the lengths and directions of the many little legs. But as it was, we were left with an opening that looked like the receiving jaws of the great fish that swallowed up Anthony Van Corlear. The error of closure, we knew, was hopelessly unacceptable. I turned to Frank. "Whadda ya think we oughta do?"

Disinterested, he began to chew on a nail. "I don't know."

"We're gonna hafta do it again," I sighed.

"Gedadda here!" said Frank.

"So what're we gonna do then?" I asked.

He walked off a few steps, then turned back. "You know that long path we spent so much time on? The one that winds all around? . . . You know, from the tunnel under the Parkway up and around Spuyten Duyvil Creek to Isham Street?"

"Yeah. So what about it?"

"So ya gotta change it. That's all."

"Whadda ya mean change it?"

"Make it go the way it's supposed to go."

"You can't do that!"

"Who says?"

"It's cheating! Besides, you gotta have some error. Or it's gonna look funny."

"So make an error. A little error."

"Jeez, I don' know . . ."

"Fa crissake, just draw the goddam path in! . . . Fix it up a little."

I kept shaking my head, not knowing what to say.

"Look . . ." Frank understood the need for patience. "If we went up there and measured it all out again, it would prolly still come out wrong . . . So, okay . . . You draw the path in the way you know it goes. Then we go back over the field notes, find the mistakes and fix'em so they match the drawing."

There was something wrong with this procedure. I wasn't at all sure about it. "Besides, who's gonna know...? What? They're gonna go up inna park and check?"

I had to admit it. Frank's long range perspective on our dilemma did have merit. I, myself, would never have thought it out that way. But I agreed, the scheme had to work.

The finished map was an artistic triumph. Everything was just where it ought to be, or reasonably close. Frank was right. The map was just fine. We passed the test, and no one was any the wiser.

36| Race Day

SPORTSWRITERS DUBBED it alternately "River Rodeo," "Driftwood Derby," "River-riding Madness." They were looking for the right combination of words to characterize the wild and wooly eastern motor boat race held each spring for fourteen years from 1928 to 1941 (then for six more years from 1947 to 1952, but limited to stock boats and motors). It was the annual Albany-to-New-York Outboard Marathon, 130 bruising miles of slaloming, slamming and shuddering down the Hudson River crouched in a "flying shingle," a "ten-foot cockleshell" a "paper-thin pancake"—names given to the lightweight hydroplanes that plied the great estuary at fearsome speeds.

In 1938 my father, Ted Roberts was the only entrant who had driven in the 1928 inaugural of this eleventh running of the outboard marathon. In his Class B boat, he, too, was the oldest at 41.

The New York *Times* reported on Monday, May 16th, the day after the race: "Blinded by a driving rain that blew almost horizontally most of the time, battered and bruised from pounding through rough water in a ten-foot cockleshell, so numb and stiff he had to be lifted from his cramped, kneeling steering position by friends at the finish and unable to walk or hardly talk for a half-hour, Roberts went through torture for 130 long miles." My father, after nine tries in eleven years, and after having been a runner up twice in 1934 and 1935, had finally won the mad dash down the Hudson. But only by a last minute reversal of fortune—happily in his favor.

Roberts about to Cross the Finish Line

Fred Jacoby, another veteran driver and winner of the race in 1935, had a fifteen-minute lead over Roberts in his more powerful Class C boat when he ran into trouble only moments away from the finish line. Rain-drenched crowds at vantage points along the Palisades and upper Riverside Drive reported seeing Jacoby's white-decked hydroplane weaving in and out of the stakes holding shad fishermen's nets off the Jersey banks. He had hugged the shore most of the miles from Albany and now had only to cut across the river to the finish line. But a peculiar accident had stalled him.

The banging up and down between each wave had broken Jacoby's drive shaft casing. The propeller still turned, but the casing attached to the steering yoke prevented him from guiding the boat. He found himself running around in circles. Finally, he resorted to an emergency measure. He braced his back against the motor to keep the propeller in a forward driving position.

With his paddle in one outstretched arm over the gunwale, gradually and almost by inches, he manoeuvered across the finish line in second place.

Roberts's Hour Finishing Time, including a refueling stop at Poughkeepsie, was 4:40:18; Jacoby's 4:41:15. It was eight minutes before the 3rd place finisher crossed the line.

Out of a field of seventy-seven starters, only 32 outboards finished the race that day. The others had either capsized, swamped or succumbed to engine failure.

The race had been scheduled to get underway at 8 a.m. from the Albany Yacht Club. It was delayed for more than four hours while drivers ballotted three times for a postponement until the following Sunday after repeated Coast Guard warnings of winds approaching gale force. But there were complications with a postponement. Additional marathons were scheduled for May 22nd. In addition, the Albany Yacht Club was not available. So at 11:45 a.m. drivers voted for an immediate start. The Class A hydroplanes were underway at 12:30.

Roberts received his William Randolph Hearst perpetual trophy and congratulations from singer Kate Smith. A week later when he had recovered fully from his ordeal he announced that he would retire from further racing.

37| Woodrow

CHARLIE WOODBURY WAS the kid who got me interested in Mt. Washington Presbyterian Church. Ten years before, Mt. Washington, then known as the Old Valley Church, had moved from the Broadway-Dyckman-Riverside Drive triangle to its new location, sandwiched in between two apartment buildings on Vermilyea Avenue, a half-block down from P. S. and JHS 52.

Woody, or Woodrow, as we called him alternately for the swing band leader or the World War president, was a square-shouldered, blond-haired kid with a high forehead, watery blue eyes and a prominent mole on his cheek. He lived with his mother, a big, rawboned woman, and his older brother whom he spurned as a pansy, a dope and a Catholic. As a widow, Mrs. Woodbury supported her two boys by working as a practical nurse. When she was home, she moved swiftly from one household task to the next and let it be known that she had no time for foolishness, especially from unruly and untidy kids. And that was probably why Woodrow tended to be stiffly matter-of-fact and direct himself. He was not given to light-hearted or subtle humor. Still, there was something warm and genuine about Woodrow which assured him a place as one of the more solid boys at the Mount Washington church and in our 8th grade class at JHS 52.

A year ago we had been reshuffled into the new junior high school program which meant that we now moved as a class from one room to another every forty minutes, to an assortment of teachers who specialized in things like algebra, science, civics and foreign languages—called in educational parlance, departmental studies. In the breakaway from the elementary grade's one-teacher, one-classroom concept, Woodrow ended up in my newly formed, now all boys class. Educators at the time had the idea that boys and girls could best be served by a clearly defined sexual orientation based upon the roles their charges could be expected to play in life. The girls were trundled off to domestic science classes; the boys to various.shops.

My failure as a Lutheran did not bother me as much as being left out when it came to the social and athletic programs the churches then offered young people. I was getting older and found myself drifting away from Ole and the Payson Avenue gang. I had fallen in with a new crowd of boys: Manny Skouros, Rudy Gehrmann, Don White, Johnny Lyden and Woodrow—all of whom were in my grade in junior high, and most of whom attended Sunday school at Mount Washington.

Woodrow assured me that joining Mt. Washington's church was the right way to go. He was forceful, clear and sincere about this as he was about most other things, and he convinced me to give it a try. He stressed that the church was putting together a basketball team and that they could use me. I have to admit, this last argument was the one that sold me.

About this time we were becoming acutely aware of our bodies and of the changes that were taking place, not the least of which was our muscular development. It was our budding manhood that now spurred an interest in the physical aspects of sports like boxing, ice skating and skiing and, of course, basketball. The church became the center for such interests because it encouraged and supported development of all kinds, not just spiritual. So with the urging of my new comrades from school I became a part of the church's program and soon enjoyed going to Mount Washington's Sunday School and Church Services. I have to stress that, more than anyone else, it was Woodrow who steered me in the path of this new righteousness. He was an ardent fellow who felt strongly about his beliefs and his ideals and who had no time for anyone who challenged them. In the same way, he was uplifted by the rough give and take of our new-found physicality.

My father had an old pair of boxing gloves at the Boathouse. Afternoons after school, Woody and I sparred until our faces were red and our sides were sore. After it was over, we both had manly, encouraging things to say to each other. He was impressed with my jab. I let him know that I felt the power of his body punches. It was at a time when we rolled up our sleeves and pulled back our shoulders to show everyone how we were becoming muscular. It meant a lot to know that you were liked and respected by a contemporary you admired. We looked, in fact, for guys of this calibre, those who stood apart from run-of-the mill types—standup guys who could be counted on.

Mt. Washington's basketball team got better with practice. We began to win the games we played with the street kids' pick-up teams. It was time for some visual sign of whom we represented. It took a lot of convincing to get the church elders to understand that we were organized now and needed uniforms. After our second season, they relented. It was agreed that we were to have sateen purple shorts and athletic shirts with white lettering. We played out a schedule of games with neighboring churches who also had organized teams, some with players much older we were, and we did fairly well against them. In the heat of play, Woodrow was always in the forefront of the action even though he was not an exceptional player. What he did do was to play hard, and that encouraged the rest of us to do the same. The result was that we often excelled as a team, while as individual players we weren't really that good.

Sunday school was no different. Where once I had dreaded the Lutheran catechism, I now waded into my Sunday school lessons with my new-found friends with joy, pride and satisfaction. Now out of knickers and into long pants, I looked forward to Sundays when I could put on my new dark green, double-breasted wool suit and march off to church with my offering envelope with the quarter inside it in my jacket pocket and my bronze attendance pin on my lapel. This was Woodrow's righteous way. It was clearly beginning to rub off on me. I liked the feeling it gave me, and I liked myself. I adopted righteousness as a way of life.

There were moments, however, when we didn't get along so well, Woody and I. As I've suggested, Woodrow was a serious sort of kid and more or less unyielding in his judgements and opinions. He took his mother to task for being hard and uncommited. He dismissed his brother as a hopeless case. And, good as I was beginning to feel with Woodrow around to light the way, I was still not convinced that it was a good idea to be so hard on people and to take so many things so seriously. Maybe there was still some of that childish carelessness left in me, but when I found ideas or situations that were too big for me to handle, I made light of them and the people who swore by them. I teased Woodrow, "Come on . . . You don't really believe that stuff about Adam and Eve and the Serpent in the Garden of Eden, Original Sin and all that . . . Come on!" I laughed and slapped him on the shoulder. Woody heated up in an instant. "So what do you believe in? You think it's funny? What's so funny? Everything's funny with you . . . Anything for a laugh, huh? Mr. Laugh-it-off . . ." And on he went until he cooled off. But you couldn't get angry with Woodrow. He was just too sincere, and it would be unkind to poke fun at him for what was really an admirable quality. I felt bad when I knew I had offended him, whether by design or accident. And then I didn't like myself so much.

Once the cold weather was on us, the manly sport was ice skating. And for this you had to have long-bladed racing skates. Nothing else would do. After four days of twenty degree weather, we waited for the word that the red ball was up at Vanny, as we called Van Cortlandt Park's Lake. This favored skating pond for the big guys was a ten-minute ride on the IRT elevated from Inwood to the end of the line at 242nd Street. We brought our skates to school with us and left directly after school.

We spent a good deal of our time on the ice showing off some new maneuver or trick: skating crouched, hands behind back; doing crossover turns; skating backwards or jumping over ropes placed at cracks to signal weak spots in the ice; or, forming a line for a crack-the-whip. I recall one time I lifted my legs for a jump and hooked the rope barrier with the long tip of one of my skates. I flipped headlong onto the ice. I lay there, out, seeing nothing but tiny lights twinkling in the darkness for what seemed a long time. When I came to, I remember it was Woodrow who was most concerned and helpful. He insisted I come with him to the first aid station in the old house where skaters put on their skates or warmed their insides with hot chocolate. Though the first aid attendant assured me that I was all right, Woodrow demanded that we quit for the afternoon and that he walk me home from the Dyckman Street train stop. I thought that this was unnecessary. It would be a long walk for him to the Boathouse and then back to his apartment. But he would hear none of it. I had to acknowlege later that this was just Woodrow's way, and it was a good way.

As we advanced in grade in junior high school and in our Bible studies in the church, it was inevitable that we should begin to see girls in a new light. Possibly we were too engrossed in boy things to have noticed or cared before. Then too, in school we were mostly separated from the girls, having been put into an all boys class. It wasn't until we shared a French classroom with part of an all girls class that our interest was stimulated. The skinny little girls we had known as little pests with fresh mouthes or, in a few cases, the okay-tomboys we allowed to play with us in schoolyard games were filling out now. Blossoming, still awkward and tentative, they were experimenting with their charms just as we were with our muscles. The magic was working. They had their eyes on us, and they soon had us off balance. We began to study ourselves in mirrors, coaxing waves into our hair and fretting over our lengthening features and oily skin. Suddenly school and church, in addition to what we had always expected these places to be, became arenas where social fencing was the new sport.

I couldn't understood why Woodrow hadn't been smitten along with the rest of us. He was as aware as well as we were that the girls were starting to look good and had become more agreeable. Yet he never expressed the least concern about this girl or that girl being pretty, nice or fun to be around. While we mooned and got silly over the charms of the lovely blonde Viola or the soft-spoken Jeannie with the "blouse-full of goodies," he sneered at us and went on in his characteristic way of casting himself as tough and unmoved. He let it be known that he was not to be taken in by such nonsense.

It wasn't until many years later that I gained some under-standing as to why Woody avoided girls. He had no interest in them because he never saw them in any way other than as infe-rior and troublesome. To put it plainly, he didn't like them very much. They made certain demands, and he would rather not complicate his life with them. This is not to suggest that he had the makings of a homosexual. On the contrary, as I found out, he took the position that girls were there to provide him with what he needed when he needed it and nothing more. For anything else in his masculine world, they were unworthy of his attention and would do well to stay away from him.

Nevertheless, Woody and I, along with the others in our little band of good guys, maintained our close-knit relationship throughout our junior high school years and beyond.

We were, all of us, finally confirmed as members of the Mount Washington church. We were proud that we were the ones who had originated its first basketball team. We attended church and were active in its Sunday evening Young Peoples' "Mizpah" dis-cussion group. I became a patrol leader in the church scout troup.

As long as these wholesome activities were sponsored by the church, Woody was comfortable and responsive. And, I should add that if boys appreciated his genuineness, girls respected him for his candor.

38| Frank 2

IT WAS THE end of June and the last day of school before the summer recess. Teachers with great deliberation and ceremony handed out report cards to excited children who looked anxiously for the only notation that mattered anymore: "Promoted to . . ."

I went off to Camp Manhattan a week ahead of Frank Wald. Camp Manhattan was one of the five, City Borough Boy Scout camps in the sprawling Ten Mile River Reservation near Monticello in Sullivan County, New York which stretched as far west as Narrowsburg near the Pennsylvania state line. Though I had moved to the Mount Washington church troop, I agreed to stay on as a bugler in Troop 727's recently formed drum and bugle corps. The Scoutmaster of 727, Al Dempster, in return got me an audition with Don McCuen, Camp Manhattan's legendary camp director. I was hired as Camp Bugler at half-tuition and the day after school closed, boarded the Short Line bus at 181st Street and Broadway with the rest of the staff, some thirty scoutmasters, waterfront, nature and craft counselors, dishwashers and orderlies.

We spent this "Pioneer Week" before the scouts arrived prying open musty sheds, sweeping away winter's debris, folding out cots and filling ticking with straw; then lugging trunks up to assigned campsites and cabins. A part of each day we listened to program directors and campmasters who outlined the season's activity schedules.

*Camp Manhattan
Ten Mile River, N.Y.
1939*

Bugling

As Camp Bugler I was quartered centrally. The troopsite's log-lettered gate spelled out: R-A-M-A-P-O. It was one of some eight campsites with regional Indian names like Mohawk, Mohican, Algonquin, Cherokee and Delaware that made up the camp. Inside the Ramapo gate six adirondack, log lean-tos spread out into a broad semi-circular pattern under the trees. A scoutmaster's tent raised centrally on a wooden platform overlooked the arrangement. Each of the sturdy little lean-tos had double-decker bunk beds, two on either side. Plump straw mattresses now rested on iron-framed springs waiting for scouts to fold out their blankets on top of them. The roof overhang extended just far enough beyond the rough board flooring to keep the rain out, and on a chilly night to draw the heat of a fire—with some of the smoke too, if the wind was right. All of Mt. Washington's Troop 757 scouts had been assigned here. I saw to it that Frank Wald would be in the lean-to I had been occupying for the last week.

The season began officially when the line of buses rolled into the camp throwing up clouds of red dust behind them from the rough, unpaved camp road. A combination of excitement and apprehension, a mid-way lunch stop at the Red Apple Rest on Route 17, and four hours of being jounced around over uneven roads did its work. Doors opened and buses reeking of vomit disgorged disoriented campers onto the camp's vast retreat field. Scouts in their broad-brimmed campaign hats, winter jodhpurs and khaki stockings and Borough of Manhattan blue neckerchiefs waited for their assignments. I spotted Paul Kroll, Billy Gassert, Marty Brink and Mickey Corelli. Then at last I saw the small dark figure of Frank Wald drop to the grass.

The provisional scoutmasters checked campers names off their rosters. I collected the Ramapo campers and marched them up the long hill to their campsite and pointed to the lean-tos where their trunks had been placed. Frank and I took one wall of our lean-to and Marty Brink and a skinny little kid who kept choking back tears of homesickness took the other.

Frank lost no time in establishing himself as troopsite observer, commentator and general wit. This new setting offered fertile grounds for comment. First of all there were a lot of things about Camp Manhattan that got in the way of Frank's casual way of disposing of things. There was the emphasis on "achievement," the campwide policing of the grounds every morning after breakfast, and then the forced-milk program: "We'll give you all you can drink . . . and more!"—by order of the camp director. Then there was the West Point style military retreat. The entire camp of some five-hundred scouts assembled by troopsites on the parade grounds each evening. They waited at attention for the blast of the cannon to signal for the bugle call and the lowering of the flags. This ceremony was followed by the march to the mess hall. The strains of Sousa's "El Capitan" blared out onto the field from the camp's new PA system.

Then too there were those camp-wide games that every scout was expected to participate in. Frank scoffed at them and wrote them off as an intrusion on his time. I guess you would have to say that Frank was never what you would call a wholesome and rugged scout or camper. He preferred a more passive, less fervent approach to scouting. He would much rather thumb through a comic book on his bunk bed or watch a garter snake engorge a live toad than enlist as a soldier on the Blue Team in the annual campwide Blue-Gold War. Nor did he derive any satisfaction from running or swimming a relay leg for Ramapo in the great Message to Garcia competition.

It wasn't that Frank was particularly unhappy or dissatisfied or wanted to change things to suit himself. He just thought it was all somewhat excessive and therefore ludicrous for Scouting to be promoted so vehemently at every turn. So he made sport of what he saw and drew satisfaction from his own version of camp life. I had to play a little tag after each bugle call I blew to identify Camp Manhattan from the Queens camp across the lake. Someone figured out words to the tag: "This is Man-hat-tan's Camp." Frank found more to his liking, "This is a kosh-er camp." Then too, Frank was stimulated by things a lot more immediate.

To get right to the heart of the matter, Frank had developed a twelve-year-old's fascination with the body, its parts and its functions. Typically, he made a betting game of comparing culinary intake with the color of the stools on the concrete slab of the troopsite's latrine, or "lala" as it was called. Next he worked out a scatological jingle for the then popular laxative, Ex-lax to the tune of the Barbasol shave creme radio commercial. And this was quickly taken up as Ramapo's fight song, much to the distress of the normally affable Ramapo scoutmaster, Bob Eastman. Then when Frank discovered that Marty Brink had an undescended testicle, he dubbed him the Ruptured Ruffian. And to poor Marty's chagrin, the name stuck. Then there was Corelli. If Corelli wasn't long on brains, his penis more than made up for the IQ handicap. And this of course led Frank to the inevitable conclusion in the matter of such proportions which, incidentally,

BOATHOUSE DAYS | 157

by his reckoning, put him ahead in the game—since his own penis was minuscule.

In the last analysis, you would have to say that if Frank was out of sync with the Teddy Roosevelt "Strenuous Life" spirit engendered at Camp Manhattan, you'd never know it from a growing number of Ramapo campers. He was dealing out stuff that was of vital concern to us. And as we saw it, he was doing it with style.

Two-weekers came and went and I always suspected that we shortened one scheduled eight-weeker's stay when we found out that the puny homesick kid in our midst was a bed-wetter. The kid had the upper bunk over Marty Brink. And that being the case, the situation was made to order for Frank. Now, let it be understood at the outset that Frank had no love for Marty Brink. None at all. According to Frank, Marty was not only a eunuch but a dirty one at that. "Lookatcha," he'd point at Marty's drooping shorts, flying shirttail, dirt-caked neck and snotty nose, "What does it matter, the kid pisses on ya? Y'd still be a schlub." Once he even tried to pick a fight with poor Marty who, not understanding, just walked away.

As for the offending kid, words of humiliation weren't enough for him. Clearly the kid had to be taught a lesson he wouldn't soon forget. It began with ritual sniffing, grimacing and head shaking. "Ya know, sompin smells in here," drawled Frank. "It's over here, I think . . . Yeah, right here." Finally, the hard evidence. The tell-tale stain on the ticking. "Och! Look at this, will ya . . . Right through the strawr an' all." Frank shook his head and sighed, "I don' know . . . I just don' know."

Now, given the right set of circumstances and with very little encouragement, kids can be creatively cruel to one another. We grabbed and "pantsed" our bed-wetter. We tied the squealing kid by the ankles and suspended him head down from a nail in the rafter at the peak of the lean-to. He should hang like this for a while, he'd get the idea. How this punishment was expected to stop his bedwetting wasn't really clear. It didn't matter. So long as the kid was wailing and flailing about in the air.

We let the kid down finally after we got through poking at him and he swore scout's honor that it was "finished, the bedwetting." The kid was gone at the end of that first two-week period and Paul Kroll from our church troop, a more or less normal kid took his place returning our lean-to to a degree of stability. In short order we settled back into the routine of camp life and the season moved along smoothly with no futher disturbances of this sort.

It was mid-August now at Camp Manhattan and I was surprised when Frank agreed to join me for the fourteen-mile hike requirement for First Class Scout. I knew he wasn't motivated by fitness or achievement programs of any kind. Yet it was true that he had helped to carve the Ramapo totem pole which some weeks ago had been mounted in the mess hall with the other troopsite totems. But this long trek through the woods? Well, maybe Frank needed to get away, free himself from the daily rigors of camp life. It didn't matter. I was glad for his company in preference to some kid I didn't know.

Some years earlier Explorer Scouts had laid out a carefully marked trail through the woods that began at the back of the camp and went to the little town of Bethel (site of the future "Woodstock") on Route 17B, some seven miles away. The campmaster at the headquarters cabin gave us a map of the trail and a penny postcard to be mailed from the Bethel post office as evidence we had hiked the full distance to the point of return. From the pantry behind the dining hall the commissary steward gave us each a ham and cheese sandwich and an orange. We looped on our canteens and studied the map. The trail was indeed well-marked and easy to follow.

It was late summer and the morning air was still crisp, a typical late summer day in the woods of Sullivan County. There wasn't much dampness in the air and the sun flickered brightly through the trees as the wind shuffled the leaves overhead. We knew it would get hot later on, but it was an ideal day for a long hike like this.

Frank and I crunched along the trail in silence enjoying the solitude of the woods and the moldy smells of the earth under our feet. We paused now and then to kick at a rotten log, shredding the damp wood between our fingers and speculating as to whether it would light up at night as "phosphorus." At times we stopped to sail a piece of shale at a trail marker. We zig-zagged across dry stream beds and climbed over downed trees until our ankles ached. Finally we felt that it was time to rest and have lunch.

We found a lichen-stained boulder and climbed up onto it. Jerking off our cord-soled Official Boy Scout shoes, we peeled away the damp socks from our swollen feet. The moist sandwiches from our knapsacks tasted good. We washed them down with the warm water in our canteens. A squirrel poised on the end of a dead branch overhead watched us. We put our socks and shoes back on and continued on our way.

The sun was high now. The air was still and much warmer as Frank and I resumed our trek. According to the map, we'd soon break out of the woods and be on the Bethel Road. Campmasters and senior scouts spoke solemnly of the woods that now surrounded us. These were the lands of the Delawares, once the stronghold of the great chief, Chingachgook. As scouts, we were admonished to be reverent. We were not exactly sure what that meant. But the thought of getting onto a paved road moved us along at a brisker pace. First, it would be easier if there was a hard surface to walk on. Then there'd be telephone poles and power lines and railroad tracks and houses and barns. Places where people lived and worked. We'd find our way quickly to downtown Bethel. There'd be stores there. Maybe even a moviehouse. Frank began to sing: "Pepsi-cola hits the spot. Twelve full ounces, that's a lot. Twice as much, for a nickel too. Pepsi-cola is the drink for you . . . Pah! Nickel, nickel, nickel . . ." He broke off the jingle blowing his nose. "How much ya got on ya?" he asked.

"Dime," I said.

"I got fifteen cents," said Frank. "With twenny-fi' cents we could get a Hoffman's Cream and two frozen Milky Ways . . . Ya wanna?"

"I'll hafta owe ya," I said, the saliva already working in my mouth. A soda and a candy bar were the quintessence of good eating for twelve year old boys.

We walked on in anticipation of rejoining civilization. However, we soon found that Bethel was not the town we imagined it would be. There seemed nothing but fields stretching out before us as we broke out of the woods and onto the two-lane paved road. We passed a few farmhouses set well back from the highway on tractor-rutted cowpaths. But mostly there were endless cornfields and pastures. As we drew abreast of them, the cows near the barbed wire fences looked up. They stared stupidly at us with their great oily brown eyes while they flicked flies away with their ears.

Some minutes later we rounded a bend in the road and were able to make out in the distance an elongated wooden structure with a flagpole. This had to be the post office from the flag, but neither of us was willing to believe it until we were directly in front of it. There was a slatwood bench with rusty nailheads backed up to the front of the dilapidated wooden building. There was a screen door and a faded sign with the words: "Bethel, N.Y." Under that, "General Store." We stared at the sign for a moment without saying a word. I grabbed at the rusted door handle and the door came open with a twang of protest, then slapped shut behind us.

Frank and I slumped down on the wooden bench outside the post office with our Coca Colas and stale Baby Ruths. The sun had dipped behind the roof as we rested in the shade. I fished my Ingersol watch out of my shorts pocket, the watch I went by for bugle calls. It said ten after two. "If we started back now and walked real fast maybe we could make swim call," I said, trying hard to lift my dampened spirits.

"Nah," said Frank absently. "It took us three hours to get here. Figure it's gonna take us longer to get back."

I pulled the soggy map from my shirt pocket and unfolded it. I held it over to Frank, pointing to the arrows, "Here's the way we're supposed to go back."

"I know, I know . . ." he sighed impatiently. He tipped his coke bottle up and drained the sudsy contents. "Gimme the map," he said snatching it out of my hands. He studied it silently.

The sun was at full strength now. The flies flitted from the empty coke bottles to the sugar on our lips.

"It's gonna be hot hiking back," I ventured dismally. "We oughta get started."

Frank tossed the map aside. "We could take the macadam road. The one the buses take to camp. It shows here on the map . . . not far from here."

I picked up the map and located the road he was talking about. "Why do that? It's longer'n the trail."

"Yeah, but it's easier walkin'," he said. "Besides, there's cars."

"What's cars got to do with it?" I asked.

"Somebody could see us. Maybe stop and give us a lift," he said offhandedly.

"Hitch a ride, you mean?" I asked.

"Not exactly," he said.

"So what? 'Exactly'?"

"I mean, if it was getting late an' we got tired," he shrugged. "Play it safe."

"C'mon, let's go." I ignored him and got up and turned to walk away.

"Ya wanna kill yourself walkin' the trail?" he shouted after me. "So okay, we'll take the trail. But figure . . . it could be dark by the time we get back."

I turned around and held up a warning finger. "Look," I said, "We're not supposed to take the road. They tole us. Besides, I don' wanna hafta to do this again . . . We take the road an' somebody from the Reservation sees us . . . We're finished."

"So they see us. So what? We coulda got lost, cun't we?"

I ignored him. "An' if we get back too early, they're gonna be suspicious."

"Yeah, an' we get back too late an' we miss supper," countered Frank.

"Aw right, aw right!" I threw up my hands weary of the argument. "We take the macadam road . . . But we walk fast. An' I'm not hitchin' no rides," I added saving the little that was left to me.

"I don' know why not," he mumbled. "Everybody else does it . . ."

I was curious to know how he came by this information. But the matter was settled and I didn't feel like pursuing it. Yet now as we walked and I thought about it, I owned to myself that taking the road was probably a good idea. To tell the truth, I was a bit tired. But more to the point, Frank had thrown a scare into me. I had a vision of us tramping through the woods in the dark, lost, tired and trying to find the trail markers. I never stopped to consider that the sun did not set until around eight p.m.

We marched purposefully for four hot miles on the macadam road until the bottoms of our feet burned. We decided to sit down in the weeds by the roadside to rest for a few minutes. A farmer in a battered Chevvy pickup truck saw us and stopped. He sensed our predicament but didn't let on. "You boys lost?" he grinned. "Hop in. I'll take you to the camp road." We didn't hesitate to accept the offer.

Frank and I jumped out of the truck at the red dirt road and took the pipe line short cut up the hill to Ramapo so as not to be seen. As it turned out we still had time for the afternoon swim. We kept our mouths shut and nobody paid us any particular notice.

Summer was over. Ten days after our hike, the camp season officially came to an end. The buses from the city were once again lined up on the parade field. There'd be lots of singing and very little throwing up now as Frank and the other campers boarded for the return trip to New York.

I was left behind with the rest of the staff to help close up the camp that now seemed so quiet and strangely empty. With the campers gone, we as seasoned leaders luxuriated in our in the lightened responsibilities and the broadened privileges we would now enjoy. We glowed with good health and good cheer, feeling very responsible and grown up. A week later our own bus crossed the George Washington Bridge and we stood up to sing the traditional "Stand Up and Cheer for Old Manhattan." Minutes later we were back on the city streets. We parted with warm messages and handshakes as we found our families. This was to be the first of many robust summers of growing up for me at the Ten Mile River scout camp. Sadly, such was not the case for Frank Wald.

The following year Frank had been signed up and was ready to go off to Camp Manhattan once again. But when Dr. and Mrs. Wald read his report card and found that he had failed French, they promptly cancelled his reservation and enrolled him in summer school. Frank was crushed. "Sixty-two! The son of a bitch failed me by a lousy three points!" He laid the blame squarely at the doorstep of Monsieur Dumont, the French teacher at JHS 52 who, it must be said, had certain idiosyncrasies that had attracted Frank's attention almost at once.

As that fateful school year had begun in September, Frank noticed that Monsieur Dumont had dandruff. There were always scales on the shoulders of his suit jacket. Worse yet, he had the unfortunate habit of brushing them off in class—usually during the daily dictée. It was this, not French that worked on Frank's mind. He linked Monsieur Dumont's psoriasis and his unfortunate habit to the notion that he was "a goddam homo." And if Dumont was a homo, it followed that French must be a fag language. Having made this determination, Frank could never bring himself to pronounce *le* any way but "lee" and *eux* any way but "ooks." Then there was that line in the little round "Frère Jacques" Monsieur Dumont had his classes sing. It was supposed to go "*Sonnez les matines.*" Frank took diabolic pleasure in bellowing it out, "Sonny laid Martina."

So, in the end, Frank's improprieties and lack of classroom decorum got the better of him. He forgot that teachers, especially language teachers listen and hear quite well. They observe too. And they rank their charges in equal measure as their charges rank them. The difference is, they hold the red pen.

This little learning experience cost Frank at least one more summer of carefree dawdling at Camp Manhattan, something that agreed with him as nothing else did.

39| Murray

MURRAY NEUMAN WAS the one kid on the Block I took an instinctive dislike to almost from the moment I became aware of his existence. He had a real smart mouth and he could get under my skin quickly and he knew it.

Murray lived in an apartment at 49 Payson Avenue with his mother and father and younger brother. Someone said that his father worked for the New York *Times* and had an important job with the paper. Mr. Neuman was a tall, straight man with a pince-nez and a waxed moustache. When he came home from work we'd watch him enter his apartment building in his dark blue overcoat, homburg hat and bow tie. Mr. Neuman always looked very imposing and very correct.

One afternoon three of us kids were playing pitcher-batter stickball in P.S. 52's smaller schoolyard after school. The batter stood in front of the white rectangle painted on the wall approximating the strike zone and the pitcher tried to strike him out. There was one fielder and we rotatated at each out. Murray, on his way home from school by the Academy Street gate, saw me swing at the ball and miss. He didn't lose the opportunity to needle me. "Give it up. You stink." I threw the stick down and walked over to him and backed him into the red brick wall. Dodging this way and that way, he kept egging me on to do something. I finally lost control and aimed a punch at his head. He saw it coming and ducked. My fist slammed into the bricks. Murray sauntered away laughing while I bellowed in pain holding onto my bleeding, battered knuckles.

One afternoon sometime later we were involved in one of those intense choose-up-sides stickball games that ran the length of the Payson Avenue hill. My team was at bat when the usual shouting match erupted over whether the long ball Corelli hit up the hill was fair or foul. All I could hear was Neuman's sharp voice coming from the outfield, rising above the rest. It went right through to some nerve inside me that was just waiting to be tampered with. I walked on out to where he was standing and challenged him to a fight on the spot. "Fight! Fight!" the other kids shouted. There was no backing out now. Both sides drifted up onto the sidewalk to watch us circle one another.

Neuman always seemed to know what I was going to do before I could do it. I aimed a blow at his head and he ducked. He caught me with a right to the side of the head. I dizzied and fell in towards him. But my head cleared quickly, and then I lost all control of what I was doing. I began to swing furiously and randomly at the body and face bobbing around in front of me. I hit him several times with heavy blows to the head. Then he couldn't duck anymore. He tried to cover up, but it was useless. I had him now and he knew it. At last he pulled away and ran into the courtyard of 49 Payson and in through the double glass paned doors to the building and up to his apartment sobbing in humiliation. I stood there trembling, the adrenelin still pumping, the blood pounding in my temples. No one said a word. The fight was over and so of course was the game. Ole walked silently alongside me down Dyckman Street a part of the way to the boathouse. As soon as I began to breathe easier he turned to go back. "You really got him good," was all he said.

That summer I ran into Murray Neuman at Camp Manhattan. I was actually surprised to see him there. It never occured to me that he had an interest in scouting. I watched him now playing first base for his troopsite in the usual after-supper softball game. He was quiet. No longer the bellicose Murray that I knew. Was he off balance learning to live with kids from other parts of the city? Was it that we both had moved ahead to this larger plan at Camp Manhattan and were no longer tethered to the Block, its protective apartment houses and the ever-watchful eye of Inwood Hill Park? I waved to him and shouted a guarded hi. He responded in kind.

Back in Inwood, Murray and I rarely saw one another since we went off to different high schools. He never raised his voice or taunted me again leaving me with no excuse to dislike him. When we did run into one another we always stopped to exchange a friendly hello and a word or two. I often thought that if circumstances had been different, we might have become fast friends.

40| Frank 3

FRANK WALD GOT to the Bronx High School of Science a half-year ahead of me. He had taken the mid-year entrance exam when it was offered at Inwood's junior high school and passed it easily. His school work had improved noticeably since that fateful year when he failed French. The experience must have sobered him up some because now he managed all of his school work quite well. Dr. and Mrs. Wald saw this and then no doubt guided Frank in the selection of the Bronx High School of Science when it came time to make a choice. Frank, they felt, could now be counted on to live up to his potential. If he had the brains—they impressed upon him—he should use them. Possibly they felt, too, that the challenges of science would further stimulate his already active imagination.

Nor was Frank opposed to the choice. This new high school would be a relief from the boredom he was beginning to feel at JHS 52. And he could only expect more of the same if he allowed himself to be marched lockstep up Fort George Hill to George Washington High School. No test was required to enter George Washington. It was the neighborhood high school. As Frank would have it, it was where the the Inwood "nebbishes" went. Clearly something inside him was telling him that it was time to separate himself from the general run.

The Bronx High School of Science was the newest addition to the city's elite high schools for boys. Among the others were Townsend Harris, Stuyvesant, Aviation Trades and Brooklyn Tech.

Temporarily housed in the the old Evander Childs High School building at 183rd Street and Creston Avenue, it was another in the growing list of city schools that specialized in something or other. In order to be admitted you had to demonstrate by a test that you possessed certain abilities, aptitudes or interests. While the content for academic courses was still governed by the State Board of Regents in Albany (as it was for all the city's high schools) the required four years of math and science was what made the difference at Science High. That, and a kind of intense dedication to restructuring the world along scientific lines in search of truths that could be relied upon.

Here, at Science High, faculty and students embraced a new kind of god. It was felt that Science and the Scientific Method were the best insurance against repeating the mistakes of the past and the one safe road to true knowledge and social progress. Europe was already at war. Now, more than ever, the world would need men who were trained to test hypotheses, men of learning who would guide the planet through these troubled times and beyond. It was up to Science to seek answers to those perennial problems that had plagued humankind from the beginning of time. Science should become the cornerstone for peace and prosperity. And we, at Science High, were being shaped to go forth with this message.

I can't say for sure whether Frank subscribed to these glowing visions. If he ever thought about them at all, he didn't say. In any case, one immediate benefit of choosing the Bronx High School of Science was that the school was a short trolley ride from where he lived—and, he could save a nickel by walking home. By the fall of 1940 when I was able to join him on this walk, it became a ritual for us to stop at the candy store at the corner of Sedgwick Avenue for a three-cent soda and two Hootens. A Hooten was a great block of cloyingly sweet milk chocolate that targeted the least hint of caries in your mouth. It was like old times again.

The Walds: Doctor, Mrs, Frank and a younger sister he called

ROBE

Runty lived in a second-story corner apartment overlooking Sherman Avenue and 207th Street. Frank's father, a stocky man whose thoughts you could read by watching the taut lines around his mouth, was a dentist. As was usual at the time, he had his office in the apartment where he lived. There was a white marble slab with black letters perched on a window ledge. It read simply: "D.M. Wald, Dentist." Mrs. Wald was a diminutive black-haired woman who had a way of pursing her lips at the mention of distasteful subjects. She worked as Dr. Wald's receptionist, assistant, and she kept his records. Frank's room was at the opposite end of the apartment from the office, by the entrance to the apartment. It was the only room I was ever admitted to, and quickly so as not to interfere with patients coming and going.

The tiny, overheated room was littered with books and magazines from the storefront Inwood Public Library just below Frank's window. There were apple cores and orange peels on the window sill waiting to be shoved into a brown paper bag and added to the dumbwaiter garbage. On a card table which Frank used for a desk there was a cigar box with radio parts in it. Alongside it sat a soldering iron and a sheet metal chassis on which was mounted two vacuum tubes, two wax-core coils and a transformer. Frank had just completed his latest project. It was an oscillator that was designed to be used with a record player and a radio in close proximity. In effect, it was a low-power transmitter.

A week or two earlier I had been involved in an earlier project of Frank's. It had involved a GHQ model gas engine that wouldn't start. We spent an entire Saturday afternoon winding friction tape around its flywheel and pulling. We were encouraged by nothing more than a teasing pop or two. Now, judging by the tangle of wires mashed into the chassis on the card table, I didn't think that the oscillator was going to work either.

Frank had got the plans for the oscillator out of a recent issue of *Popular Science* which was sold at school along with the progressive, however short-lived evening tabloid, *PM*. I helped him pick out the components the week before at the Lafayette Radio store on Fordham Road near Webster Avenue. He spent four-dollars and sixty cents of the money he earned washing the family Dodge for a bagful of coils, resistors, capacitors, hook-up wire, a transformer and tubes. He mounted the parts on a make-shift chassis of sheet metal left over from an old JHS 52 shop project. Following the pictorial diagram in the magazine, he completed the wiring.

I watched now as Frank twisted the two wires from the phono arm to the oscillator inputs. He set Glenn Miller's recording of "Tuxedo Junction" on the turntable and tuned his old portable radio to an unused frequency at the upper end of the AM band. He fiddled with the oscillator tuning coil and the tuning knob on the radio. The radio emitted a squeal. Frank worked it down to a rumble and found the music. The phono needle had just reached the doot-dat part of the selection's arrangement. He looked up at me. Crude as it looked, the little transmitter actually worked quite well.

I began to spend more time at Frank's now. On certain eve-nings, I'd have questions on my geometry homework that only Frank could answer. Afterwards, I'd stay on in his room and, using the oscillator hook-up, we'd play swing records from our growing collection.

One night we tried an old carbon mike I found at the boat-house with the oscillator. By a switching arrangement Frank devised, we were able to announce the records we played. This opened up the way to a whole new level of experimentation and general dallying which did, sort of, come under the heading of "science."

We did radio skits and then began to work out racy chatter for remote broadcasts featuring dance bands. These were take-offs on the kinds of things that were actually done on late Saturday night radio . . .

"And now from the roof garden of the Hotel Pediculosis on the Bowery overlooking New York's littered sidewalks, we bring you the tantalizing rhythms of Del Tremens and His Spasm Boys . . . Right now the boys are just itching to get going with 'I Got It Bad, and That Ain't Good.'"

We were in love with words and taxed them to their limits.

All this was great fun for a while. Then it occured to us: who was there to listen to and appreciate the clever stuff we were dealing out?

Now, Frank had often complained about the people in the apartment next door. It seemed they had a big console radio with a speaker that boomed. It often annoyed him while he was doing his homework. One night I had come to Frank's for help with my geometry homework when the radio was on. We stopped to listen. Judging from the sound, the radio must have been set against the same wall that separated the neighbors' living room from Frank's bedroom.

We had an idea. If we moved the oscillator over to the common wall, we'd have it within a foot or so of the loop antenna of their radio. If the tuning screw of the oscillator could be tuned down far enough to reach the lower frequencies of the broadcast band, we could cut in on their listening. It was worth a try.

Crouched on his knees, holding the little transmitter in his hands, Frank worked himself over to the wall. I guided the wires and moved the record player from the card table to the floor. I put my ear to the wall and listened while Frank fiddled. It was WABC, 880. The Lux Radio Theatre was presenting a radio adaptation of *Our Town*. Emily had just come back from the dead to replay her twelfth birthday when both of us heard the squeal. Frank adjusted the screw and the whistle lowered to a rumble. Then all sound disappeared entirely. We had pre-empted the network's program. Frank and I grinned at one another. We were on the air!

We opened with our version of *The Shadow*. Lamont Cranston had just entered a nudist colony. MUSIC—UP AND UNDER.

Unhappily, the one thing we overlooked was, if we could hear the neighbors' radio through the wall, they could hear our amplified music and racy banter. Our experiments in creative broadcasting often grew loud when we got carried away. Within minutes of our taking control of the neighbors' radio, the buzzer to the Wald apartment sputtered. Footsteps passed by the door to Frank's room. The apartment door opened. We could hear voices echoing in the hall. It was a woman and a man. They hated to complain but . . . sure the boys didn't mean any harm . . . Now it was Dr. Wald's voice: . . . very sorry . . . will look into it right away . . . won't happen again.

We didn't have time to clear all the stuff off the floor before Dr. Wald burst through the door to Frank's room. He sized up the situation in an instant and the lines around his mouth tightened. "What the hell's the matter with you guys!" He aimed a kick at the oscillator in Frank's hand. Fortunately it missed. "Now get this goddam mess cleaned up . . . And no more of this nonsense. You hear?" Muttering an obscenity, he turned and left, banging the door shut after him.

We closed the station down in silence. It was a shame. Everything had been going so well. Did accepting responsibility mean that you had to give up all the things in life that were fun to do?

41| Bobbi

IT WAS QUITE by chance that I ran into Bella Abrams on Isham Street that afternoon after school. She was walking her scotty dog by the curb. She had changed so much that I didn't recognized her—except for her eyes. They were still big and round and blue, just as I remembered them. Immediately the name Puddles came to mind. But of course I addressed her as Bella. But she told me quickly that her name was Bobbi now.

We drifted along aimlessly trying to stay free of the dog's leash and filled in the years we hadn't seen one another. We recalled those first days in school and particulary her embarrassing experience. It seemed so long ago, that day she disgraced herself and wet the floor in front of her classmates. She could laugh about it now, but at the time it was mortifying. It took her a long time to get over it she said. I believed her.

We were in our second year of high school now. Bella, or rather Bobbi was at Walton, an all-girls school. She was sixteen and spoke in a soft voice that was pleasant to listen to. I remembered her club legs. They were gone now with the rest of her baby fat. She went by the name Bobbi, she told me, because she could never stand the name Bella. We exchanged talk about high school and found that we were pretty relaxed with one another. Then it suddenly occurred to me that I needed a date for my high school's Spring Frolic dance the following week. I asked Bobbi on the spot if she'd like to go with me. She had to ask her parents she said, but she was sure it would be all right.

I rang the doorbell to Bobbi's apartment. She was ready and waiting at the door. She was wearing a blue-green print dress and carried a light coat over her arm. Her glistening black hair was rolled under at the nape of her neck in the fashion of the day. She had fixed a gardenia by her right ear. She smiled at me as we headed for the elevator. Was this the same girl I once knew?

The sidewalks radiated the smell of an evaporating rain. It had been a warm, humid day with late afternoon showers. We strolled leisurely over to the trolley terminus at Broadway and 207th Street and waited for the conductor to change the trolley poles and reverse the direction of the wooden seats in the X-car. The car was open now and had sides of wire-mesh. Winter's windows had only recently been replaced.

Bobbi and I sat quietly by one another as the car groaned its way up the hill to University Heights and onto Fordham Road. We were comfortable with one another without talking. Maybe it was those shared secrets that drew us together. I breathed in the warm spring air. I sensed that it was going to be a relaxed evening with this lovely girl that I had just rediscovered.

I was earning no laurels at the Bronx High School of Science. I was an average student who had trouble keeping up with the rest. I was only a fair swimmer on the swimming team. I knew few boys well at the school. There were a handful of us from Inwood and a few others I knew from Camp Manhattan. But most of the boys came from the Bronx, and the majority of these were Jewish. I was just another presence in this one's chemistry class or in that one's French class.

But now at the Spring Frolic, suddenly everyone knew me and wanted to talk to me. It was as if I'd become a celebrity between the day's classes and the evening's festivity. Part of this had to be because of the change in setting—the break from the daily grind of the classrooms and the lavishly decorated gym we were in right now. But more of it, I suspected, had to do with Bobbi. Katz, Lowenstein and Gerber looked past me incredulously. "Where'd you find her?" one of them whispered at me while Bobbi sipped at her strawberry punch. "Jeez, she's gorgeous!" It crossed my mind that they were Jewish and intuitively knew that she was too . . . and what the hell was she doing with a *goy* like me? No, I decided. That's stretching a point. She was just an attractive girl and would be to anyone. Being Jewish had nothing to do with it. I wondered what they'd say if I told them that she was simply a kid from Inwood. We'd known each other since first grade at P.S. 52. "Well, see . . ." I imagined the words, "she was this kid—Bella is her real name. One day she stood in front of the class and peed all over the floor. She couldn't get herself to say her lines in the class play!" I took it all in feeling pretty smug knowing that Puddles and I had come a long way from that awkward moment. We danced the Lindy and the slow fox trots. She followed my lead easily. As expected, my newfound friends cut in.

It turned out to be the fine evening I expected it would be. My date had created a sensation. I flushed in the afterglow as we rode the elevator up to Bobbi's apartment. I wanted to pull her to me, to kiss her right then and there. But this, I knew, would be unacceptable. It would send out the wrong message. I would kiss her goodnight at the door. That was the way. But there was something bothering me. I sensed that she felt it too. It couldn't have been the memories of those first awkward days at school. Those were intimacies we treasured. Was it something about being Jewish? Something that I was not privileged to understand? But how could that rule out an innocent expression of affection? I had to try. I made a tentative lunge at her at her apartment door. She turned aside. Not angry, just smiling. Then it came to me. I understood that it was better to leave things the way they were: a wonderful evening, unpunctuated and uncomplicated. One that would keep another fond memory in tact.

42| Wolfgang

IN 1938, AT the age of eleven, Wolfgang Spitzer and his mother and father escaped from Nazi Germany and sought refuge in the United States. It was time for Jews, those who had the money and the influence, to get out of the Third Reich.

The small family with not much more than the clothes on their backs made their way into New York Harbor, then moved into a three room apartment at 49 Payson Avenue. They appropriated the needed articles of furniture from fellow refugees who had settled in Inwood and who had led them there.

The Spitzers had been well off in Germany by any standards. They had owned several apartment buildings in Berlin. Along with their possessions, these were among the many things they had to leave behind when they arranged passage to the United States. There was another son too, older than Wolfgang, who was mentally retarded. It was not possible to secure his release from the authorities in time. Sadly, he had to be left behind with relatives. He never did get here. Understandably, the family spoke little about him. Hitler's plans to expunge the Fatherland of all manner of "inferior" beings were all too clear.

Wolfgang's father was a stumpy little man with a keen wit. He was well-educated with a doctorate in Philosophy from Heidelberg University. With his parrot nose, wire glasses and long cigar, he could have posed for pre-war, brownshirt anti-semitic posters. Dr. Spitzer quickly found work through a New York connection. It was with a firm that published comic books. It was

a come-down from the kind of publishing he'd been doing in
Berlin. But it put food on the table. Wolfgang's mother soon helped
to provide needed income too. A nervous woman, who alternated
between raging at and pleading with her son, she devised and
marketed a mail order item. It was a birthday candle with deco-
rative annular rings that were numbered. A parent was supposed
to burn it down ritually a year at a time at each birthday from age
one to twenty-one. (She would boast proudly some years later
that Mamie Eisenhower had bought one.) As for Wolfgang, he
was duly enrolled in the 7th Grade in JHS 52 and learned his
English quickly by spending his afternoons and weekends in
Inwood's movie houses and by listening to the radio at night.

Wolfgang's passion for boating soon brought him and his family to the Boathouse. They were looking for a canoe for Wolfgang,
one that he approved of and, of course, one that his parents
could afford. Between Missy's maddening attempts at German
and the family's broken English they finally managed to arrive at
an understanding. They bought a used Old Town canoe for
Wolfgang for fifty dollars and and he became a familiar figure at
the Boathouse.

Wolfgang, from the beginning, wanted to move in all the right
circles. Partly, that meant that he wanted to do and be all things
American. He made every effort to efface his past and he let it be
known that he didn't want to talk about it. He mumbled one or
two words and guarded responses to anyone who asked him questions. He shouted his mother down when she spoke German to
him when there were Americans present. (Yet, she was still *muti*
to him.) And, pretending ignorance, he withdrew at any mention
or discussion of Jews or the Jewish religion. Nor did he seem
concerned about what was happening to Jews in Europe. It was
as if these subjects were forever banished from his conscious-
ness. For his friends, Wolfgang singled out kids he knew who
would not pry into, or remind him of his past—and, kids who
were willing to teach him the new ways.

Wolfgang was short and compactly built. He was possessed

of an inner anxiety that moved him constantly. By his own admission, he did not sleep well at night and preferred to be up and doing. Also, he also suffered from severe migraine headaches. I once watched him curl up into a ball under the deck of a sailboat. He locked his hands around his head and whimpered to be put ashore.

Wolfgang could be arrogant too. But his was the kind of arrogance that was carefully tailored to the environment and the individual he happened to be confronting. He never wanted to offend anyone who could help him get ahead or from whom he could learn. If there was a disagreement between him and his associates, he would usually back down—especially before those he had selected as his mentors. Yet, with his mother and father he could be ruthless, often times turning savagely on them. Outside the home, he directed most of his arrogance to people he judged to be subserviant and of no particular importance to him. A waiter at Broger & Luessen's soda parlor once delivered a milk shake to him in place of the malted milk he ordered. It was an innocent mistake. Wolfgang erupted immediately. "I didn't order that. Why do you bring me that? Didn't you hear me what I said?" While he may have been trying to impress the people he was with, he succeeded only in embarrassing them. And Frank Wald was quick to pick up on this failing.

To Frank Wald, Wolfgang was an unprincipled and pushy little wretch. One afternoon when Wolfgang was on the river in his canoe Frank and I took the boathouse skiff and challenged him to a water fight. It was spur-of-the-moment stuff and Frank was at his creative best with language which, incidentally, he forgot carried quite well over the water. Leon splashed as I rowed by. "Have at you, teutonic mongrel," he bellowed. "Arrogant hun bastard. We'll teach you your place here . . ." Pass after pass we crossed by one another chopping our paddles into the murky water. Frank was more vituperative and profane at each pass. This went on until we were all soaked. It was all in fun, and Wolfgang had to laugh. Yet here was Frank in rare form unloading on Wolfgang in a way that no one would mistake for fondness.

It was inevitable that Wolfgang at some point would have to change his name. As soon as he realized that he had a distinctly German first name, he changed it to William. He asked that everyone call him Billy, or Bill from now on. Those of us who continued to think of him as Wolfgang often found this hard to do. We still remembered him as that fawning little tag-along in grey woolens. While we never admitted it, we now had a weapon we could use on him. By calling him Wolfgang we'd remind him and others who he really was and where he came from. It was unkind, though maybe, at times, needed. Especially on those occasions when "Bill" got cocky and turned on those who had helped him when he first arrived here.

Wolfgang, at about the same time as he changed his name, decided that being Jewish was also a needless handicap. It was just another painful reminder of the past. Through us, Frank, Woodie, Rudy and me, he began to make himself known to the young people at Mount Washington Presbyterian Church. Soon he was attending Sunday School classes there. He was agressive and eager to help whenever there was a bazaar, a picnic, or a rummage sale. His persistence paid off too. In a short time he was accepted as someone who could be counted on, a regular. Soon no one remembered, knew or cared where he came from. And that was exactly the way he wanted it.

Although it was a long subway ride from his Payson Avenue apartment, Bill was accepted at and attended Brooklyn Tech High School. It was the next to the last step of his coronation as an all-American. Bill had only to finish high school now and he could add that final touch. Soon after the war ended, he enlisted in the Army of the United States.

43| Algie

ALGIE KOOPMANS WAS shorter than average at fifteen, but he was compact, full-chested and muscular—a bantam kind of kid. He was fair-skinned and had fine brown wavy hair that cropped neatly to his head with one stroke of the comb. He also had regular features with good strong teeth that he displayed willingly each time he smiled, commonly after he'd made some pointed remark. While the rest of us moaned over our acne, Algie had perfectly clear skin. In fact, the only thing that interfered with his good looks was his glasses. But the frameless, octagonal lenses he wore blended so well with his features that he actually looked hollow-eyed when he took them off.

Algie had not been a product of P.S. or JHS 52. At some point he seemed simply to materialize at Mount Washington Presbyterian Church, and then at the Bronx High School of Science. We later learned that his family, consisting of his step-mother, step-father and baby sister had moved to an apartment on Nagle Avenue from Southampton, Long Island. By his own admission, Algie hated New York and longed to return each summer to the farther reaches of Long Island, the place he knew best and considered his real home.

I never knew anything of Algie's place in his family, or exactly why the family moved to the City. First, his surname name was Koopmans, but the family name was Spoletto. He claimed to be of Dutch origin, yet the woman he referred to as his mother and his step-father were clearly of Italian descent. With their olive skin, black eyes and black hair, no one would question that. I came finally to believe that Algie was probably orphaned at an early age and was taken in by this family.

Another thing about Algie's family that didn't mesh was that his people had apparently earned their principal living in service occupations at Southampton's fashionable beach clubs and resorts. Algie looked for opportunities to show anyone the snap shots he'd taken of a frowning Gary Cooper while he was working as a beach boy at the club where his mother and step-father also worked. But in New York, his step-father , he said, worked as a figure skating instructor at the Ice Palace adjoining Madison Square Garden on 50th Street and Eighth Avenue. This didn't fit at all. And if it hadn't been for the free passes he gave us for Saturday afternoon skating sessions where we were able to watch him at his work, I wouldn't have believed it. On top of that, Mr. Spoletto was outspoken about male figure skaters. "Homos" he called them. Leading us to wonder how he came to be a male figure skating instructor.

Algie was not a very good basketball player, but he was a scrapper and he played hard. He was a regular on the Mount Washington team because he fought for the ball and, having gained possession of it, was always willing to pass it off to one of the taller players to shoot. But there were some problems. Algie was easily inflamed and ready to fight at any provocation, real or imagined. Whenever he was on the court we were prepared for fights to break out, and as soon as this happened, we called him to the sidelines to cool off. He never objected. He regained his composure quickly and was soon back in the game.

This same quick temper displayed itself in school too. I watched him in the 5th floor cafeteria one lunch hour get into an argument with Joe Horowitz, a summer staffer with me at Camp Manhattan. Before the dispute could get to the stage of a shouting match, Algie hit Horowitz in the mouth sending him backwards over a table. Nobody was ready for it, it happened so fast. But it was over that fast too. Algie had got it out of his system and simply walked away leaving Horowitz with a bleeding lip and everyone around him stunned.

Nor was conversation one of Algie's fine points. He complained incessantly about anything and everything while you listened, or pretended to. If I happened to meet up with Algie after school we'd walk back to Inwood together. While I didn't shun his company, by the time we got to Jerome Avenue my mind began to wander as Algie babbled on about some problem he'd faced in study hall or in the chemistry lab and what ought to be done about it. Once he was launched into his tirade there was no stopping him. If you disagreed with him or challenged him, he was offended and righteous in his indignation. I discovered that it was better to let him drone on and say "yeah" every so often. While he bleated away, at least I'd be free to daydream until we parted by the IRT subway stop at Nagle and Dyckman. When his prattle became unendurable, I'd make some excuse and continue on up 207th Street to Broadway.

As such, Algie was not the kind of person you'd imagine girls would take to—and as far as we could see, they didn't. While Frank, Rudy and I were experimenting with the Inwood girls we knew from JHS 52 and Sunday school, Algie never gave the slightest indication that he was interested in girls. Of course he'd be along on church group outings and picnics, and he'd participate in the activities. But he never favored one girl over another, nor did they show any interest in him. That was why we were dumbfounded when Danièle Duchamps came along.

Dany Duchamps dropped into our midst from another planet, and suddenly our Inwood girls paled by comparison. It was hard to pinpoint what made her so attractive and appealing. It could have been the tailored clothes she wore, or maybe the ease with which she wore them. Maybe it was the charming way she had of mixing in with boys. Possibly it was her doe eyes, or the symmetry of her face. Or, was it the graceful lines of her body or the refinement of her speech? Whatever it was, all three of us, Frank,

Rudy and I were smitten—completely gaga over her. Even Algie blurted out that she was "pretty nice."

Above all, Dany was sociable. She had no qualms about having a couple of boys in her apartment after school when there were no adults at home. In this way, one afternoon we found out that she was of French and English origin, and that her father was a classical musician. She volunteered that while her mother was English, she had been brought up in Paris. She and her mother and father came to the United States when she was twelve. She spoke French at home, she said, but had been grounded in English early enough as to have no French accent. She was, none the less, admittedly French at heart and showed us with pride the chalk-like death mask of Napoleon perched on a shelf behind the grand piano. While she looked upon us merely as *copains*, she had each of us accusing the other of making a fool of himself as we tripped over our feet trying to impress her.

We never understood why, nor were we ever clear about how it happened, but late one spring afternoon a gang of us were playing seven inning choose-up ball at the Tubby Hook landfill ballfields along the Hudson. Algie was with us, but didn't want to play. He was a poor player because of his eyesight. Aside from Ole's sister, Alma and her girlfriend Ginny, we noticed that a few other girls were sitting on the benches watching us play ball. Sure enough, one of them was Dany . . . and she was sitting with none other than Algie! There he was, jabbering away in his flamboyant, gesticulating way, and there she was listening. We finished our game and the crowd left and straggled back up Dyckman Street. Algie was still talking. And now we noticed that he and Dany were holding hands! It was utterly incomprehensible.

On a Friday night a few weeks later a "carny" had set up in the usual place on the fields along the Speedway south of the old Sherman's Creek cut. There was an attractive kind of seediness about a carny that made every teenaged kid in the neighborhood want to be there. It was the tree from which hung the forbidden fruit. If you could pick up a couple of girls there, you could probably convince them that they ought to take a walk with you along the parkside under Fort George Hill. Stopping in the shadows of a tree to kiss the girl was the object of that maneuver. We knew it and so did the girls.

This particular carny night was special because someone had said that the girls from "Lady queen-a-martice," as we called it, would be there. They were fresh-mouthed, but they were good-looking.

Four of us drifted through the grass alleyways, stopping here and there at a booth to pitch pennies at a fishbowl, or to throw baseballs at a pyramid of aluminum milk bottles not more than ten feet away. As good as you aimed and as hard as you threw the baseball, you could never seem to get all the bottles off the shelf. Woodrow failed, so did I, then Rudy. Each of us bought a candy apple for a nickel and teased Woodrow into testing his strength with the maul-and-gong, knowing that he'd fall short of the bell. Then Rudy, Frank and I tried it. We all tried it again and again, but never quite made it. We sauntered on through the crowds nodding to the familiar Inwood faces, but didn't find the girls we expected.

It was nearing ten o'clock and we'd spent all our money. All the girls we'd seen were either too old or too young or with other guys. The evening was a bust, but why not walk back on the park side and check the action? We passed bands of little kids darting here and there who should have been in bed, and older couples holding hands and drifting along absorbed in conversation. "Wait a minute," Frank stopped dead. There in the shadows ahead were the silhouettes of Algie and Dany. Giddy and giggling at one another they were holding hands, dancing around a tree. We stood motionless watching as Algie jumped for a branch and pulled himself up. He reached down for Dany and she came up alongside him on the branch. He went on up the tree and she followed. Well-up in the tree, they found opposing limbs to sit on where they could see one another. And there they sat, just staring into each other's eyes. Not a word passed between them. "Crazy," said Frank. "They're absolutely crazy!"

None of us could figure out Dany's sudden loss of aplomb. What would that comely girl, that cultivated classic beauty want with a dolt like Algie? He could get her to climb trees and go gaga with him, but she wouldn't so much as go to a movie with any one of us. What magical spell did he use on her to make her behave in this unseemly way? What was it that Algie had that we didn't?

Of course, we never found out. At the time such things were beyond the limits of our understanding.

44| Peggy

FRANK, RUDY GEHRMANN and I were feeling the urge to get out of Inwood, to find some "new blood," as we put it. By this we meant new girls. There was the general sense that Inwood's girls knew too much about us and we knew too much about them. Familiarity was beginning to breed . . . well, let's just say restlessness.

We had heard that roller skating was a good way to meet girls. The Kingsbridge Roller Rink under the el on Jerome Avenue was a few blocks north of the Fordham Road trolley stop. It was a large rink and the one closest to us. Word had it that there were loads of girls there, especially on Friday nights. So one warm Friday night early in May we decided to give it a try.

We were finishing our first year in high school and girls were increasingly on our minds. We'd had our appetites whetted the year before by a junior high graduation dance and those rough-house June afternoons with the Inwood girls at the Miramar Salt Water pool at 207th Street and Tenth Avenue. But we were still awkward and unsure of how to handle ourselves—especially with girls we didn't know.

At the roller rinks we'd heard that there were Couples Only skating times. A boy had only to single out a girl during the intermission and ask her to skate with him. Meeting new girls this way was simple, direct and relatively painless. The girl either said yes or she said no. This basic protocol made it a workable forumula for us who were still struggling to find appropriate approaches. It was how I met Peggy that Friday night.

I spotted her from across the rink holding herself by the railing, a pleasing rather slim figure, not too tall, with blonde hair that touched her shoulders. I made my way over to her. Did she want to skate the Couples Only with me? She smiled OK. I took in her face, her wide-set eyes and broad smile. Then I noticed the heavy powder she'd used to lighten the redness of her acne . . . Jeez, I thought, her face is as blotchy and pimple-ridden as mine! For a moment I felt embarrassed and uncomfortable. But the feeling left me quickly as we glided around the rink to the organist's music and I felt the firmness of her waist under my hand. We were kindred sufferers, but with one important difference: she was a girl and I was a boy.

I found out on that first Couples Only skate that her name was Peggy and that she went to Roosevelt High School. She lived a block off Fordham Road on Decatur Avenue. I couldn't help but notice that she was shy and almost as awkward as I was in this new situation even though she managed to conceal it better. Her voice was soft and she answered all my stiff questions directly without hesitation and with a smile. But she never volunteered information on her own or asked me any questions. I took her to be a quiet girl, and that was all right with me.

By the second Couples Only skate we were more comfortable with one another and it was tacitly understood that we were going to be together for the rest of the skating session. I waved over to Frank and Rudy. They understood the situation and left us alone.

It was eleven o'clock and the organist played a goodnight, ladies medley for the last All Skate. I asked Peggy if I could take her home and she said yes. We boarded the trolley for the short ride to Decatur Avenue then walked to her apartment building two blocks in from Fordham Road. It was a brightly lit moonlight night and we sat on the stoop at the entrance to the building. The air was cooler now and I decided I could risk putting my arm around Peggy. She didn't pull away. I can't remember whether we said anything to one another or not. If we did, it had to be about what we liked and what we didn't like, and we must have been pretty much in agreement. At one point, I stopped talking and thinking about things to say and leaned my face over and kissed her. She responded. Her lips gave way as they met mine and something stirred in my insides. I held onto the kiss and pulled her closer to me. She finally drew back from me and smiled her great, wide smile.. I was lifted to new heights. Boy, this was something. Here I was at last, really necking with a girl!

Flushed with my success, I went on kissing Peggy until two o'clock in the morning. Then my legs cramped and I had to stand up. Suddenly I felt a sharp, stabbing pain in my groin. This must be the "rocks," or "blue balls" some of the older boys at school talked about. Bent over at the waist, I took her hand and asked if I could see her again. She smiled and said yes. I memorized her phone number and headed for the trolley stop, wiping the caked lipstick from my mouth. Under the street light I looked at the handkerchief . . . Okay. Here was the proof: the victory and the purple heart of my encounter. I'd show it to Frank and Rudy tomorrow.

I waited a good half-hour for the trolley to come. By the time I got back to the Boathouse it was three o'clock in the morning. There, sitting in the lamplight of the living room, were my mother and father in their bathrobes. The questions began to bombard me: "Where were you? Do you know what time it is? We tried to find you everywhere. We called the Walds. They had to wake up Frank. He said he thought you were with some girl. We called Mrs. Gehrmann and Rudy . . . Nobody knew where you were. Why didn't you call? Do you know what time it is? We were worried sick about you. We even called the police . . ."

I let the questions fly by. There was no room for answers anyway, even if I had been willing to offer any. What was I going to say? "Well, see, I met this here girl at the roller skating rink and her name was Peggy . . . And she had pimples too, just like me. So I took her home, see? And I got to kissing her and I didn't

want to stop . . . And for once I forgot all about the goddam time
and who would be worried." What I did say was that I was sorry
and that I didn't mean to upset or cause anybody any concern. I
just lost track of the time . . . They seemed stunned when I said
I was tired, and, without so much as an excuse me, turned away
from them and went directly into my room closing the curtained
French doors after me.

45| Frank 4

RUDY GEHRMANN'S PARENTS were German-born and had emigrated to the United States shortly after World War I. Rudy's father had been a U-boat sailor in the Kaiser's navy, and Rudy's understanding of German culture was based on a little story his father liked to tell: The junker captain admonished his green crew: "Ven on der boat, you say nodding. You don't speag undil you are spogen to. Und, ven you laugh, you laugh militarische, 'ha, ha!,' und stop."

Rudy had just been put into my class as a new kid when I introduced him to Frank Wald. It was in JHS 52's great schoolyard one lunch hour. It was the same year Frank had had the trouble with Monsieur Dumont and French.

Rudy looked long at Frank and then asked a question that I thought was strange. "This guy a Jew?" he said. He said it loud enough for Frank to hear him. "Yeah . . ." I stammered, unwilling or unable to put together a thought by way of a better response. It wasn't the kind of thing you said when you first met a new kid. We all came to know about one another's backgrounds soon enough. Then we used the information to goad or provoke. But Rudy's question came ahead of time and out of the blue. It was both abrupt and belligerent. I wondered what was behind it. Frank took it without lifting an eyebrow. But while his facial expression didn't change, something was going through his head: *Could it be true? They don't know any better.*

Some time later I learned that Rudy and his mother and older brother, Hans were forced to move from Home Street in the Bronx into a smaller and cheaper apartment in Inwood. Rudy's father had died unexpectedly of a burst appendix. The doctor somehow didn't, or couldn't get to it in time. And the doctor happened to be Jewish.

When we moved on to high school, the three of us Frank, Rudy and I drifted loosely into a friendship that I would have to say was based mostly on shared interests of kids our age. Rudy went to De Witt Clinton High School and the three of us would meet after school in the candy store under Frank's apartment. It was a block away from where Rudy lived at the corner of Sherman and 204th Street. Two Harry James hits, "Music Makers" and "Sleepy Lagoon" unexplainably penetrated and moved something inside us. We played them on the great Wurlitzer juke box again and again waiting for the parts that seemed like pure magic to us. Rudy, who had learned how to smoke at Clinton, would buy a couple of "loosies." Then we'd move on to the listening booth at Irv's appliance and record store at 207th Street near Broadway. Here we could listen to the latest hits for free.

After an hour of listening, the air in the small booth grew damp and stale. Irv, who lisped when he got excited, banged on the fogged glass and sputtered, "For crithake, buy thumpin or get out!" But we knew he really didn't mean it the way he said it. He liked having kids around. One of us would buy a record just because Irv was a good guy. He was tolerant where others often weren't. I remember one afternoon Frank made one of his clever remarks to the trolley motorman just as we jumped off the car at his stop. The motorman reacted instantly. He bounded after Frank leaving the car right where it was. Frank ran, but the motorman caught him after a few steps. He spun Frank around and clapped him across the mouth. He didn't say a word. He just walked calmly back to his trolley as if nothing had happened.

One afternoon the three of us drifted down to the Boathouse and began to sift through the pile of old Vocalion and Cameo records. We looked in vain for something our ears could identify with. The sound from these records was tinny and the rhythms vo-do-de-o jerky. They were mostly all from the twenties, not like the new recordings, the ones we knew about. I remembered my father said, "Take 'em. Get rid of 'em."

We acted on that. We found a string of firecrackers left over from the 4th of July. Frank fixed a firecracker in the hole of a record and handed it to me. I cocked my arm. Rudy lit the fire-cracker and I sailed it out over the river. We frittered away the entire afternoon watching the records blow apart in the air one after the other until at last they were all gone. With adolescence plaguing us, there was still some of the boy left in us.

When Rudy first moved to Inwood, he began to attend Holy Trinity Church on Cumming Street. Later, he decided to change to Mount Washington, mainly because Woodrow and I had told him that we had found a home there. Soon we were all in the same Sunday school class together and went to the church services that followed. For reasons that weren't clear to us at the time, Frank would meet us outside the church after Sunday school. Rather than have him just hang around, we invited him to attend church services with us, that is, if he would like to.

During the service we watched him with a degree of curiosity. Maybe he knew we were watching him. Anyway he responded where the congregation was called upon to respond. He sang the hymns with us. He dipped his head in silent prayer. He even contributed an offering. But during the sermon he began to fidget and whisper. He found some of Dr. Hadley's remarks amusing and volunteered some amusing parallels, not all of which were in the spirit of the sermon. With a reproachful look from Rudy or me though, he'd leave off. One Sunday after church services I asked him point blank why he didn't go to his own services at the synagog. I knew he had been bar mitzvahed and kept the high holy days with his family. But Friday nights or Saturdays he was always ready to join Rudy and me in some social activity or other. Frank was evasive and embarrassed whenever the question of religion came up. He drawled, "Ah don' know. We're not very religious, I guess," and let it go at that. Judaism and being Jewish was a subject he never willingly discussed, though I knew it was not because he was ashamed of either.

Along with our other new interests, clothes and grooming seemed very important to us at the time. To be dressed properly in the fashion of the day, a high-schooler ordinarily wore covert cloth wool pants, pleated and with high waists. The cuffs had to be pegged, but not too close, around the ankles. The jackets were long and of the three-button, single-breasted type. The fully padded shoulders tapered down to a tight fit at the hips. Also a light tan raincoat soon became the schoolboy rage. The coat was worn as an all-weather coat. But it was never to be buttoned. The sweater underneath it with the school colors and letters had to be seen. Rudy's raincoat, like his smoking, was an announcement that he had left off being a snot-nosed kid.

Frank for his part, by careful negotiation with Dr. and Mrs. Wald and Alexander's on Fordham Road, began wearing an oversized (he would grow into it) muted green-orange glenn-plaid jacket with brown covert cloth pants. Fully dressed, he wore a green paisley tie he called an "embryo tie" with his oxford cloth white shirt. But it was that jacket though that set off his ensemble.

The long, wide-shouldered, tapering jacket, later further exaggerated to become a part of the zoot suit, was what dance band musicians wore. When Frank saw Tex Beneke in the Glenn Miller band at one of those twenty-five cent Saturday afternoons for high school kids at the Hotel Pennsylvania's Cafe Rouge, he quit the fiddle for the sax immediately and began seeing himself as a Tex Beneke type. His new jacket fit the image well. Sax players had a way of hunching up their shoulders, squaring them off for a "solo ride." Frank's shoulders were naturally square, and the fact that the jacket was too big for him added to the effect. It made him look stocky . . . hep. But it also paved the way for ridicule. Rudy and I, time and again, had ritual fun at Frank's expense. We stood on either side of him and on a signal pressed the sleeves of his jacket in underneath the shoulder padding.

"Whoa-ho! What's this?" we bellowed. "Look . . . at . . . this!" He'd shake us off without comment and walk away.

Sometimes the three of us would go to a movie. Frank's natural way of drawling his words made it easy for him to mimic the dry, raspy delivery of radio comedian Fred Allen whom he idolized. When the film began to bore him, he interpreted the action for us as Allen might have, ridiculing the scene. At times, he anticipated dialog or turned the words around just after the lines were spoken. Often as not his parodies were funny and we laughed. Frank naturally took this as encouragement. He bantered on until Rudy leaned over and told him to shut up: "Whaddya go to the movies for? To make smart remarks through the whole goddam picture?" Frank would settle back for a time, but then he'd begin again. This time the shut-up-dammit was accompanied by a sharp punch on the arm which Frank responded to immediately with a punch of his own. These exchanges never went beyond that though. One of us not involved in the encounter would say, "Come on, you guys. That's enough, huh?" It stopped there. We watched the rest of the movie in silence, and the sullenness wore off.

When the Gehrmanns moved to Inwood it was for reasons of economy, but they still found it hard making ends meet even in the new, smaller and cheaper apartment. Widowed Mrs. Gehrmann, a jolly wall-eyed little woman, had to take work as a cleaning lady in downtown office buildings. Hans, or Hal as he preferred to be called now outside the family circle, left school after the ninth grade to take work as a day laborer. To further help, Rudy, as soon as he could and until he graduated from De Witt Clinton, worked after school. At first he took a job as a Western Union messenger in midtown Manhattan, then as stock boy in Gimble's department store basement. During the Christmas holidays he worked full time at the General Post Office at 33rd Street. The Gehrmann apartment, small as it was still had three bedrooms. Eventually, Mrs. Gehrmann rented out one of the rooms to an elderly woman acquaintance, but only partly as an accommodation to her.

As they grew older, the Gehrmann boys watched out over their mother who in her turn cherished them. In the midst of hard times, loyalty and family pride pulled the small family closer together. Each felt a responsibility to the other, and each accepted his obligation without complaint. Possibly because of the closeness that developed, they were still able to make light of most of the difficulties they faced daily. They struggled and they managed. They complained little of their hard lot and still knew how to laugh. You knew this right away if you happened to be among them on one of those rare occasions when the whole family—aunts, uncles and cousins gathered together to celebrate a birthday or some holiday. As a casual caller, I was pulled right into their midst as though I were some sort of long-lost relative. As I thought about this later, it occurred to me that Frank Wald, who knew and saw Rudy as much as I did, had never met anyone else in Rudy's family. As it turned out, he'd never set foot in the Gehrmann's apartment, even though he only lived a block away. I never knew whether it was because he consciously avoided the Gehrmanns, or because he was never invited.

As we grew older, it was ever clearer that Frank and Rudy were headed in different directions. That old Jewish canker continued to fester inside Rudy. When Rudy and I were alone, Rudy often complained about Frank: "The Jew . . . Always horning in, always forcing himself on you. You can't get rid of him. Sticks to you like he was glued." Maybe only dimly aware of Rudy's continued prickliness on the subject of Jews, Frank never really considered whether he was wanted or not. He took it for granted that he was. While he may have been disturbed by awkward silences and sidelong glances, he wasn't going to give in and make any concessions just because he happened to be Jewish. It never mattered before. Why should it matter now? All he wanted was to enjoy the company of a few friends his own age, kids he'd grown up with and with whom he could share his ideas about music, clothes—and of course, girls. What the hell did being Jewish have to do with that? And what possible difference could it make?

Still he exercised discretion. He had already learned to ignore, if not understand, what he had no control over. *Don't pay any attention to them.* He was philosophical about Hitler and the Nazis until we entered the war. He claimed no kinship with the Jewish refugees who had escaped from Germany in the late thirties and found their way into American schools. At times he found their arrogance (in the person of Wolfgang) no different from the "master race" they were lucky enough to escape from. If Rudy or I unwittingly passed a remark that was blatantly anti-semitic, he'd let it go by without comment. *What can you expect?* In some insidious way, the carefree give-and-take of childhood was being replaced by social distinctions that, in the end, would have to set us apart as adults.

One overcast fall afternoon in our final year of high school, Frank, Rudy and I took the Boathouse skiff and rowed across the Hudson River to Palisades Interstate Park. We dragged the small, flat-bottomed boat up onto the sand and walked the shore line north of the ferry slips to the deserted picnic grove. Here there were wooden benches and tables and open fireplaces for the picknickers. And centrally located, there was a small stand that in season sold soft drinks, ice cream and candy. Except for the wash of the ferry at the shoreline, everything was quiet. The season was over and the stand was boarded up. We walked over to it and I leaned absently on one of the panels. It gave under the pressure of my arm. "Hey, it's open," I said.

"Nah," said Rudy examining the crack. "The hook is missing is all."

"I wonder if there's anything in there?" I said.

"Could be," said Rudy. "A little shove and this hook'll go. It's pretty loose . . ."

Frank had been monitoring our conversation. "Whyancha just leave it alone," he said.

"G'head," I said to Rudy, ignoring Frank, "give it a shove." I remembered the cocoa raids on the Camp Manhattan commissary.

"Fa crisesake, no! Leave it alone!" shouted Frank. "What the hell's a matter wichoo guys?"

"What're you scared or something?" I said to Frank. "There's nobody here. We're just gonna see what's inside."

Rudy had popped the hook loose and was holding the panel up. He lowered his head and peered into the darkness. "Sh'I go in? Whaddya think?" he asked.

"G'head. I'll hold it fa ya," I said. Rudy slid over the countertop and dropped to the plank floor beneath it.

"That's breaking-in entry!" shouted Frank, serving notice. "I'm going back to the boat." But he didn't. He stood watching us with his arms folded over his chest..

I held the panel further up so Rudy could see better. "Anything good in 'ere?" I asked.

"Jeez, yeah," said Rudy, "They left a lotta stuff. They're prolly still open on week ends . . ." He nodded over to where Frank was standing. "Lookit him. The jew is worried. He's shittin' in his pants."

"Hey,Frank. C'mere," I beckoned. "Looka what we got here."

"Gedadda here," said Frank.

"I'm gonna grab some of this stuff," said Rudy. He began stacking up on the counter Mary Janes, Tootsie Rolls, Hershey bars, chewing gum and packs of cigarettes.

"That's stealing!" Frank was pointing an accusing finger. "What're you guys, nuts? . . . I don't want any part of this." He turned and headed off toward the skiff.

Inside the stand, Rudy was singing: "Wissel wile you woik . . ." He whistled like the seven dwarfs did in the movie, continuing to thump around on the board flooring, collecting and stacking. I filled my pockets and the inside of my shirt with the first load and headed off for the skiff.

"Here," I said to Frank, pushing a handful of the small packages at him. "Stow them under the bow seat where it's dry."

Frank shook his head from side to side. But somehow he felt compelled to do as I asked. "This is bughouse . . ."

Suddenly I caught a glint, something moving in the distance. It was a car, a '41 Plymouth coupe. I recognized the familiar radiator grill. Then I saw that the car was black and white . . . Jesus, a cop! My mouth went dry. The patrol car was rolling slowly along the lower road, heading right for the stand.

I emptied my pockets quickly at Frank. Hands in pockets, I adopting a rolling gait to make it look less like running. I got to the stand seconds before the police car did. I eased around to the blind side by the opened panel. Inside, Rudy was trying to sound like Vaughn Monroe, then Curly : "Racing widda moon . . . Nyuk, nyuk."

"Shut up!" I hissed. "A cop!" We got the panel closed just in time. The cop had got out of the Plymouth now. I heard his shoes crunching in my direction. He came around the stand and stopped in front of me.

"What are you doing here?" said the trooper. "The park's closed."

"Oh yeah? I didn't know that." I tried to sound casual. I pointed at Frank who stood frozen by the skiff. "My friend and I, we rowed over." The trooper moved closer to the stand. He peered at the cracks in the side panels and began poking at the boarding. He returned to the counter where I was leaning. "Get away from there," he said.

I didn't move at first. Then the expression on his face changed. Something in his eyes said: you better move your ass or else. I moved aside. His trained eye found the corner of the sprung panel. He lifted his head to warn me don't move, then pushed with both hands. It was just enough of a shove to dislodge Rudy from his perch on the counter top inside where he had been frozen. It sent him thudding onto the floor of the stand. The trooper held the panel up high with one hand and spotted Rudy, eyes wide open, an unlit cigar in his mouth. The trooper's free hand went automatically for the thirty-eight at his side. "All right, you . . ." said the trooper, "Get out of there."

Rudy was dazed. He lifted himself to his feet and rolled over the counter top through the opening made by the trooper. Off in the distance Frank slumped dejectedly against the side of the skiff waiting for the inevitable.

The three of us sat on the hardwood bench in the small cage waiting. The sergeant at the Alpine barracks beckoned us out one at a time and questioned us at his desk, typing the information onto a form. We waited some more. Twenty minutes later another officer brought us sandwiches and coffee. Frank ate the food like it was chalk. Except for the end of his nose, he had gone gray.

Now, Rudy and I were taking this all in, and pretty lightly at that. It was a new experience. And the only thing we could relate it to was the prison movies we'd seen where inmates rattled tin cups against the bars shouting, "Yah, yah . . . Lousy screws . . . The food in'is joint stinks!" We had found something to laugh about.

The sergeant rounded the corner to the cage. He looked at Frank and saw that he was miserable. Then he looked at Rudy and me. "You think this is funny?" He waited. We hung our heads and smiled at the floor. "Look at me when I talk to you. And get that smirk off your faces." The voice was cold. "We don't play games here. You been charged with breaking-in and theft. Those are felonies." Frank groaned. "I'm not sure what the judge'll want to do with you guys." The sergeant's voice softened. "A lot could depend on how you choose to regard this." He looked at each of us in turn. "Give that some thought."

When the sergeant judged that he had made his point he asked, "Which of you is Wald?" Frank choked on the words: "I am." "We called your home," said the sergeant. Your father will be here in a little while. You're going to be realeased, all of you, into the custody of your parents pending a hearing a week from today." He found the right key and unlocked the cage. "Mr. Wald said he'd drive each of you home." He led us back to the front office and motioned us to the bench to wait.

Dr. Wald was masterful in his handling of the situation. He

listened attentively to the sergeant, nodding in agreement now and again to indicate that he understood. When the sergeant was finished Dr. Wald said: "You're absolutely right, sergeant. I can't imagine what these guys were thinking about . . . I guess they really didn't understand what happens when you break the law." He made sure we heard what he was saying. "Maybe they didn't know that a police record stays with you for the rest of your life. Maybe then they wouldn't have done what they did . . . They acted stupidly and without thinking. I believe they know this now. And I think they'll want to pay for the damages . . . I also think they'll want to apologize for the trouble they caused you . . . and for being wise guys."

Dr. Wald didn't say a word until after we had crossed the George Washington Bridge and followed the streetcar tracks down Broadway to Inwood. "You guys are a bunch of dopes, you know that? . . . Psss.." He kept shaking his head from side to side.

My father had towed the skiff back to the Boathouse by the time we arrived. He and Dr. Wald exchanged a few words. Both men laughed about something they had in common. My mother and father had very little to say to me the following week. I knew that this meant I'd have to take whatever was coming to me. With Mrs. Wald, though, it was a different matter.

When she learned what had happened, Mrs. Wald found it hard to keep her composure. How could Frank allow himself to associate with such morons? Street bums with no brains at all . . . Criminals! "And you," she flung at Frank, "You're the worst of all . . . Why? I'll tell you why. They commit a criminal offence and you end up with a police record." She put special emphasis on the next five words: "Because—you—were—with—them . . . Nice, hah?" Inconsolable, she began to weep. Through her anguish and tears she managed to blubber out, "And the sad part . . . the sad part is, you know better . . ." In the end, she lost control entirely. "You're never to see that bum Rudy again, do you hear what I'm saying to you?" How I escaped her wrath I'll never know.

Mrs. Gehrmann had been upset too. But she hadn't really understood too much of what Rudy told her. All it meant to her was that Rudy was late and he'd have to get his own supper if he still wanted anything to eat. She was tired and was going to bed. A half-hour later Mrs. Wald phoned and got a half-awake Mrs. Gehrmann on the line. Angrily, she told the story of the whole sordid business from beginning to end, prefacing each stage with a "Did you know that . . ." Her interpretration left no doubt that Rudy had been the instigator and the sole perpetrator of this criminal mischief and therefore ought to be the one to suffer, not Frank . . . "And now, just because he happened to be there, Frank has to have a police record . . . Let me ask you something: is that right? Do you think that's right?"

Mrs. Gehrmann, as she listened, became more and more unhinged, not sure of what she was hearing. Alternately, she kept calling out for Rudy to come and shouting back into the phone, "No, no . . . My Rudy's a good boy!" At last, she began to sob and quake. Rudy had to pull the phone from her hand and hang it up.

Frank agonized well beyond the hearing and its happy resolution. He was choking on a dilemma not of his making. He accepted full responsibility for his role as an accomplice in the candy stand caper (as we later called it) and had been willing to pay his share of the damages out of his allowance. He never pointed an accusing finger at Rudy or me for implicating him in what was clearly our juvenile mischief. And he was very angry with his mother for lashing out at poor Mrs. Gehrmann. She shouldn't have done a thing like that.

He was unhappy with himself too. He tortured himself that he *did* know better and yet did nothing except protest mildly. How could he have allowed himself to get into such a muddle in the first place? It was dumb, the whole thing. But how could he know what was going to happen? It wasn't planned. What more could he do to stop Rudy and me than he did? Sure, take the boat and start to row off. They'd come after him, realizing he meant business. The whole thing would never have happened. But he couldn't do that to his friends. It always came back to that: his friends . . . *You don't need friends like that.*

The image of his parents flooded over him. It was like they were waiting, always waiting God forbid he should unshackle himself from their expectations of him. What was so goddam bad if he wandered off a little, strayed from the path of righteousness once, just once? Did he always have to be where he was supposed to be? Do what he was supposed to do all the time? To drift, to change his plans, to wait and see what happens . . . That wasn't allowed. Always he had to report in, to chronicle, to use the right words, to justify, and above all . . . to be smart. It was as if his movements were immutably fixed at birth by some ancient tribal law, the greatest commandment of which was: "Thou shalt not be a dope." Ach, the hell with it . . . He left it at that.

46| Missy 5

MISSY AND WEST separated from one another by some arrangement that was never revealed to me in any great detail. I had to piece the story together myself. Then the reason for the separation became clear as I grew older.

In the beginning, there were the arguments I had witnessed as a child: the questions and the accusations and the denials. Then, West turned up at Huntington Beach less and less often. And when he did, it was usually only to gather up a few things—most often, the art supplies he needed. West too, hated confrontations. He got in and out of the house as quickly as he could before Missy was able to collar him and ask him questions; then vent her anger over being left alone to tend to the business of maintaining two households. But West's irresponsibility was only a by-product of something larger. The dispute, as it had been from the beginning, was really over West's dalliances with a string of mystery women.

First there was the Russian woman. West had begun to book passage to England yearly. He gave as his reason that his parents were growing old and had requested that he come more often to see them. Now, Missy was either not invited to join him on these trans-atlantic crossings or declined to go. Very probably, she felt an obligation to help out at the Boathouse and to see to the Huntington Beach house. This, of course, was made to order for West. In any case, West didn't go abroad alone. Friends who saw him off at the Cunard Liner pier remarked that the same woman was always standing by his side at the ship's railing. While she was never fully identified, one of the small group waving bon voyage recalled seeing her with West at a party in Greenwich Village. Her name was Natasha and she had a Russian accent. Beyond that, nothing was known of the woman.

Then Missy learned that, while she was at the Boathouse, West was bringing a woman to the Huntington Beach house on summer weekends. The neighbor in the house across the road reported seeing a blond-haired woman. West had explained to them that she was his sister. "Your sister-in-law's been coming quite regularly," the neighbors told Missy. "She was here just last week." The thing was, West didn't have a sister.

West had also got into the habit of phoning my mother to find out whether Missy was at the Huntington Beach house or in the city at the Boathouse.

Missy didn't say anything to indicate that she was angry or upset by all these reports, but it soon became clear that she was not going to let this business go on forever. She became more and more irritable with the tenants at the Boathouse. When my mother tried to tell her about the things West had been doing, Missy told her to mind her own business. She even lost her patience with me when I rode my bicycle through the main house and out onto the dock of the Boathouse screeching to a stop before going over into the water. It all came to a head late one winter afternoon.

West had phoned the Boathouse from the 14th Street apartment saying that it would probably be better if Missy stayed at the Boathouse for a day or two. He had come down with a strep throat and didn't want to give it to her. He had the doctor look at it. He'd be all right, just needed to rest in the apartment by himself and take his medicine. The following day Missy decided that she had better look in on West. If she had any suspicions about West and this business of a strep throat she kept them to herself. But we noticed that she didn't phone ahead before she left the Boathouse and headed downtown on the subway.

Missy went down the stairs to the tiny basement apartment and unlocked the door with her key. She turned the corner of the vestibule that opened out on the studio living room. There, lying on the day bed cradled in West's arms in a slip was a young woman. Missy didn't wait for words. She seized the arm of the girl and pulled her to the floor. Then she picked up the girl's pumps and grabbed the clothes that had been carelessly thrown over a chair and dragged the girl to the front door. She lifted her up and slapped her on the back of the head with one of the pumps. The girl was too surprised and stunned to do anything. Missy freed a hand and reached ahead of her opening the door to the apartment. Then she kneed the girl in the backside sending her sprawling onto the landing outside. "Slut!" was all she said.

Breathing hard, Missy wheeled and went back into the apartment. She marched over to the day bed where West was now slumped, his head in hands. "I'll be back for my things in the morning." She pointed a finger at him. "Don't be here if you know what's good for you." Missy left without another word, stepping over the girl who was still trying to dress herself on the landing. She climbed the steps to the sidewalk and headed for the subway.

West recognized the futility of his situation. He knew that the time had come for him to bow out of this marriage. Still, he felt that it ought to be done gracefully. Or at least as gracefully as he, for his part, could arrange it. He phoned Missy and asked for a few minutes, for a brief meeting with her at the Huntington Beach house. On the phone, he got her to agree to a civil discussion of the terms of their separation. He needed only to collect a few personal belongings from the house. She could keep all the other stuff.

It was over and done with in a few minutes. Missy gave West her key to the 14th Street apartment. West found the key to the Huntington Beach house in his pocket. He presented it to Missy with one final touch of panache: "It's all yours, M'dear." He picked up his suitcase, went down the path to the driveway, got into his Ford and drove up the hill and out of Missy's life.

Missy did keep the Huntington Beach house. West signed over his half of it to her. She lived in it, as she had before, during the winter months and rented it out in the summer months while she stayed at the Boathouse through the boating season. She was lucky enough to find a responsible tenant who rented the house year after year. She never returned to the 14th Street apartment. And life went on without West.

One night a year or two later the telephone rang at the Boathouse. We had just finished supper. My father got up from the kitchen table and went to his desk in the living room to answer it. It was a woman's voice: "Mr. Roberts? . . . Is this Theodore Roberts?"

"Yes," my father replied. "Who is this?"

"That doesn't matter," said the voice. "Is your mother Caroline Westmacott?"

"Yes . . ." my father answered tentatively.

"And was she married to a Bernard Westmacott?"

"Yes . . . Who is this? What's this about?" asked my father.

"I've been asked to call you by Mr. Westmacott's sister . . ."

Ah, not that sister business again, thought my father.

"Mr. Westmacott died this morning," the voice went on. "His body has been taken to the City morgue on Staten Island."

"What?" said my father. "Who is this anyway?"

"That's all I can tell you," said the voice. "I'm sorry." The connection clicked to a dial tone.

My father came back to the dinner table. He sat down slowly, stunned. He was visibly shaken and unable to get a word out. "What's the matter? Ted?.. Ted, what is it?" said my mother. She had to pry the story out of him.

"All right. Calm down," she said. "West is dead and he's at the Staten Island morgue . . . You have no idea who the woman was who called?"

"No," said my father. "She wouldn't say."

"And that business again about West's sister..?" said my mother.

"I know," said my father. "That's what I can't figure out."

"Well, it's obvious, isn't it?" said my mother. "It must have been the same woman he was bringing with him to Huntington Beach. She must have been with him when he died."

My father looked confused.

"Look. You've got to call the morgue, said my mother. "And if this story is true and not some kind of a cruel joke, you've got to let Missy know."

The Staten Island morgue was indeed holding a body whose name was verified to be that of Bernard Westmacott. He had died two days ago as the result of a coronary thrombosis according to the attending physician who signed the death certificate. He had been in the care of a woman who said that she would inform the family. She was not implicated in the death in any way, and asked that her name be withheld. Formal identification of the remains by a family member would be required before the body could be released. That would be a . . . Mrs. Caroline Westmacott, purported to be Mr. Westmacott's estranged wife.

My father phoned Missy at the Huntington Beach house. He told her about West's death and all that he had learned and what they needed to do. He asked her to get an early morning train to New York. He would pick her up at Penn Station and they would take the ferry out to Staten Island together and identify the body.

At first Missy protested. "I don't see why I should have to have anything to do with this," she fumed. "The man made it clear how he felt about me. Let *her* take care of him."

"We can't do that, Ma," said my father. "You're still his wife, legally . . . I know how you feel. But this is something we still have to do."

West's face looked emaciated, not as either of them remembered him. Missy and my father gazed as if paralyzed at the still, bloodless face before them for a moment, then nodded to the attendant who directed them to the outer office.

The man at the desk spoke matter of factly. "Who will be claiming the remains?" He waited pen in hand.

"No one," said Missy, flatly.

My father looked up at her dumbfounded. "You can't do that, Ma . . ." he finally said, looking hurt.

"Why not?" said Missy. "What did he ever do for me?"

"He deserves a decent burial," said my father quietly.

"Then let that woman bury him then," said Missy. "I don't owe him a thing."

The clerk interrupted. "The City requires that the remains be claimed for burial by a family member . . ." He stared at Missy for a moment. Missy's expression remained unaltered. "In lieu of that," the clerk continued, "the remains will be buried by the City for a charge of sixty-dollars . . . Is it your intention to claim the body, or to have the City bury him?"

Missy reached into her pocketbook. She opened her change purse and came out with two twenties and two tens that had been neatly folded in half. "Here," she said to the clerk slamming the bills onto the counter. "Throw him into your Potter's Field. That's all he'll get from me."

My father was deeply disturbed by the incident. He kept repeating while shaking his head, "What a waste . . ." He would look at my mother as if searching for some answer. "He was a talented man, an educated man . . . To throw his life away like that." I suddenly understood that my father was genuinely fond of West. I was never sure of the relationship between the two men. But as I thought more about it, it became clear to me that West was the only father my father had known. He had loved and respected the man for the guidance and the part he had played in his life.

Missy never spoke of West again. She held onto the Huntington Beach house for six more years from the time West returned his key to her. Then she sold it to her faithful tenant.

47| Frank 5

THE WAR DIDN'T catch up to Frank Wald for nearly a year after he graduated from the Bronx High School of Science. He had gone on to NYU's School of Engineering while the Wald family made plans to move to Endicott, New York. After a dismal semester at the University Heights campus where he demonstrated that engineering was not for him, he left the City with his family for the greener parts of central New York.

The Author in 1943

In the summer of that year I hitch-hiked down to Endicott from Ithaca where I was a Navy student at Cornell University. It was late in the season, and the Walds were proud of their Victory Garden. "Runty" had grown several inches, outgrowing her brother's nickname for her. Dr. and Mrs. Wald showed me around. They were pleased to have me stay the weekend with them in their new home, a seventy-year old farmhouse to which a dentist's office had been added. The rest of the afternoon was left to Frank and me. It was warm one for August, and there would be enough sun left for us to see a little of the countryside.

We walked a mile or so along a back road and laughed as we recalled our days at Camp Manhattan and our abridged fourteen-mile hike. Frank asked about Rudy. Did I hear from him? Yes, I had a letter. He was in the Navy too, a Pharmacist's Mate somewhere in the Pacific attached to a Marine division. Frank motioned to a cowpath. We followed it to the bank of a rock-bottom creek. There was a deep spot under a willow tree. We stripped down to our underwear and lowered ourselves into the water and continued to talk about the changes that had taken place in our lives since we left Inwood and the city behind.

At the dinner table Dr. Wald talked about the importance of the trace minerals in the garden vegetables we were eating. He complained about his new patients, rurals most of them, who didn't take care of their teeth and had "mouths like sewers." Mrs. Wald was maternal and cordial. She had little to say herself, but found better ways to say what had already been said by some-one else. After dinner she and "Runty" saw to it that I had what I needed; we listened to the radio shows and went to bed early.

Some months later I received a letter from Frank. He had been drafted into the Army. He had tried for the Navy, but had been rejected because of his eyesight. I had one more letter from him with an A.P.O., Boston address. He had just finished com-munications school and was waiting to be shipped overseas. He was taking the Army to task: "They got a way of making every-thing more complicated than it is . . . Everything's got to be regulation. By the time they figure out how it's supposed to be done, it's either too late or already done."

One night in our wardroom, the captain on the converted World War I destroyer I was assigned to recalled the words of a flag officer he had overheard. The admiral was irritated by the way a fleet operation was being conducted. "Gentlemen," said the admiral, "it occurs to me that we are winning this war by the sheer preponderance of force and materiel." Maybe it was just the choice of words, but we all laughed. Frank Wald came immediately to mind. I wondered where he was and how he was faring at that moment.

48| Nexus

The war was over. Most of us drifted back to the old neighborhood and tried to catch up with what we left behind. But things didn't seem quite the same somehow. The institutions that made up our old Inwood had changed, and were continuing to change fast. The Dyckman Street ferries with their old walking beam engines and side-wheels suspended operation sometime during the war for the duration. They never resumed their regular crossings of the Hudson. They were replaced by a makeshift passenger ferry for a time. The trolleys with their tracks and overhead wires that once laced the Bronx, that began for us at 207th Street and Broadway, were being torn up and replaced by buses. The classic Albany-to-New York outboard marathon returned for a few years But with stock boats. The flimsy flying shingles never came back.

Of the old Inwood crowd, the girls we left behind had grown up. Out of school now, most of them worked. They wore the New Look and heavy make up. They were looking for husbands, those of them who were not already married. They were more than pleased to go out with us, and not necessarily for old times' sake.

And, in Inwood now there were street gangs made up of younger brothers left behind to fend for themselves while dad or big brother was away, and while mom worked at a defense plant.

Mt. Washington, too, had a new pastor. We went back there to join the Men's Club so that we could shoot pool for free while we readjusted to civilian life. Our readjustment was helped along by a government stipend known as the "52-20 Club" ($20 a week for 52 weeks), or college enrollment under the G.I. Bill.

The face of Inwood had changed. To live there we had to adjust to it Doing the old things, the familiar things with the old familiar faces didn't work for us anymore. Nor was the old neighborhood quite as fulfilling as it used to be. Maybe it was just no longer possible for us to live there.

Soon enough we realized that we couldn't go back and had to go forward. Inwood, as we saw it now, was just too small, and we wanted to get out of it. We wanted to go to new places, to do new things, to find new people. And that meant that we had to have cars. So we bought fifty-dollar pre-war junkers off used car lots and replaced main bearings, radiators, carburetors and distributors and made them run. And when they did run, we drifted out well beyond the old neighborhood, finding grander places and a larger way of life.

In the end, we recognized that the time had come for us to move on. And sooner or later, all of us did. Of the old place, the Inwood that we once knew and our tenancy there, only the shadows remained. They were trapped in time. But in being left behind, they were not alone. They mingled with all of the other shadows that were left there before them.

_/_/_/

Bibliography

Abbott, Wilbur C. *New York in the American Revolution*. New York: Charles Scribner's Sons, 1929.

Barlow, Elizabeth. *The Forests and Wetlands of New York City*. Boston: Little, Brown and Company, 1969.

Bloom, Jennifer K. "What to Do with Sherman Creek? The Fight Is On" New York *Times* 29 Jan, 1995, XIII—CY, 7:1.

———. "Rebirth Seen for Decaying Pier" New York *Times* 29 Jan, 1995, XIII—CY, 7:1.

Bolton, Reginald P. "Guide to the Named Streets and Avenues of Washington Heights, Inwood and Marble Hill." Reprint, New York: *The Commonwealth Weekly*, 1914.

———. *Indian Life of Long Ago in the City of New York*. Port Washington,N.Y.:reissued by Kennikat Press, Ira J. Friedman, Inc., 1971 (first published, 1934).

———. "Indian Notes and Monographs: A Series of Publications Relating to the American Aborigines." vol. 2, no. 7. *New York City in Indian Possession*. New York: Museum of the American Indian, Heye Foundation, 1920.

———. "Inwood Hill Park on the Island of Manhattan." New York: the Dyckman Institute, 1932.

———. *Washington Heights Manhattan – Its Eventful Past*. New York: the Dyckman Institute, 1924.

Bormann, Edward J., ed., "The Story of Mount Washington— Silver Jubilee Supplement—1932-1954." [Private Printing] Inwood-on-the-Hudson, New York City, 1954.

Calver, William L. "Recollections of Northern Manhattan." *New-York Historical Society Quarterly*, 32-1 (1948): 20-32.

Davita, Albert. "History Comes Alive in Inwood." New York *Daily News*, 25 Nov. 1974.

Dembart, Lee. "Inwood Hill, Uptown Wilderness." New York *Times* 28 Jan. 1977.

"Dyckman House" W. H. *Arts Quarterly*, Fall and Winter, 1984-85, p 6.

"The Dyckman Valley—Yesterday and Today" (Anniversary Edition). Mimeographed. New York: P.S.152 Manhattan,1960.

Flexner, James Thomas. *States Dyckman—American Loyalist*. Boston: Little Brown & Co., 1980.

Goetz, Robert F. "If You're Thinking of Living in Marble Hill" New York *Times* 19 Feb, 1989.

Gray, Christopher. "Encrusted Relic of a Mid-19th Century Inwood Estate" New York *Times* 5 June, 1988.

Henderson, Helen W. *A Loiterer in New York*. New York: George H. Doran Company, 1917.

Inwood Chatter, 4, 1 (Jan. 1946) Mimiographed. New York: Inwood Junior High School.

Irving, Washington [Diedrich Knickerbocker]. *A History of New York* . . . New York: 1809.

Ivins, Molly. "A Renaissance in a Forgotten Neighborhood." New York *Times*. 9 Oct. 1981.

Jackson, Kenneth T., ed. *The Encyclopedia of New York City*. Yale University Press, New Haven & London; The New-York Historical Society, New York, 1995.

Jameson, J. Franklin, ed. *Narratives of New Netherland* 1609-1664. New York: Charles Scribner's Sons, 1909.

Kass, Sarah A. "If You're Thinking of Living in Inwood" New York *Times* 23 April, 1989.

Kenney, Alice P. *Stubborn for Liberty – The Dutch in New York* . (A New York State Study) Syracuse, NY:Syracuse University Press, 1975.

Kieran, John. *A Natural History of New York City*. New York: The Natural History Press, 1971.

Kilpatrick. van Evrie, ed. "Fiftieth Anniversary of the Inwood School—P.S. 52, Manhattan, New York—1858-1908." *New York: New-York Historical Society*, n.d.

Local History Collection *Kingsbridge Historical Society*. , [ca. 1850—1965]

Knight, Walter David, ed., "The Story of Mount Washington—1844-1932." [Private Printing] Inwood-on-the-Hudson, New York City, 1932.

Mc Cullough, Esther Morgan, ed., *As I Pass, O Manhattan*. New York (?): Coley Taylor, Inc., 1956.

Moscow, Henry. *The Street Book. (An Encyclopedia of Manhattan's Street Names & Their Origins)*. Hagstrom Company, Inc., NY, 1978.

"Native American Festival in Manhattan" (photograph) New York *Times*. 15 Sept, 1991: M,34

New York (N.Y.). Dept. of City Planning. Manhattan Community District 12: Washington Heights, Inwood / City of New York, Department of City Planning. New York, N.Y.: The Dept., (1985), c1984.

New York City Guide (American Guide Series). Reprint, Octagon Edition. New York: Octagon Books, 1970.

(American Guide Series) New York: Random House, 1938.

Peck, Richard. "Inwood—Old Dutch, New Latin." New York *Times*. 7 Aug. 1977.

"Petition for a Public Park at Inwood Manhattan Island." Mimeographed Extract. *New York: American Scenic and Historic Preservation Society*, May, 1904.

Riker, James. *Revised History of Harlem (City of New York – Its Origin and Early Annals*. New York:. New Harlem Publishing Company, 1904.

Revkin, Andrew C. "An Oasis Appears on Dyckman Street" New York *Times* 7 July, 1995 B, 1:4.

Ruttenber, E. M. *History of the Indian Tribes of the Hudson River (Their Origins, Manners and Customs...)* Reprint. Port Washington, N.Y.: Kennikat Press, 1971.

Spies, Francis F. *Inscriptions from Graveyards in Yonkers & Inwood,* N. Y. Mount Vernon, N.Y.: Spies, 1925.

Stokes, Isaac Newton Phelps. *The Iconography of Manhattan Island,* 1498-1909. New York: R. H. Dodd, 1928.

Van Zandt, Roland, ed., *Chronicles of the Hudson – Three Centuries of Travelers' Accounts.* New Brunswick, N.J.: Rutgers University Press, 1971. New York: New York History Company, 1892.

Yarrow, Andrew L. "Exploring Inwood Hill's Urban Wilderness." New York *Times,* 1 May 1987.

_/_/_/